First Published 1981
First Edition 1981
Second Edition 1981
Third Edition 1981
Fourth Edition January 1983
Revised Fifth Edition May 1983
Sixth Edition July 1984
ISBN 0 9507777 0 6
© Toshiba (UK) Ltd

Typeset by PAD, London 01-854 2580

Colour reproduction by NHK Offset Plates Ltd. Birmingham.

Printed in England by James Cond Printers Birmingham.

TOSHIBA Book of Microwave Cooking

Annemarie Rosier

Home Appliance Division
Toshiba (UK) Ltd.
Frimley, Camberley
Surrey GU16 5JJ

Acknowledgements

Book design and colour illustrations by Ed Perera

Photography by Lawrence Ellar

The photographs in this book were taken in the Home Economics Kitchens of Birds Eye Walls Ltd., Walton-on-Thames, Surrey. Toshiba wishes to thank the Company, its Chief Home Economist, Mrs Ann McWalter and her staff for their co-operation in making this possible.

Equipment for photography supplied by:

Lakeland Plastics
Microwave Ovenware Ltd.
Thorpac Ltd.
Pearsons & Co (Chesterfield) Ltd.
Anchor Hocking
Alcan Polyfoil Ltd.
The Kitchen Shop, Weybridge

Contents

Welcome to Microwave Cookery

Welcome to the exciting new world of microwave cookery. We know you will enjoy using your new oven and will soon be wondering: "How did I ever manage without it?" Your microwave oven can be used either for producing food on its own or in conjunction with other pieces of equipment — your cooker hot plates, the grill, the oven itself or a deep fat fryer. But however it is used you will find your food tastes fresher, looks better and is generally more appetising. Once you get used to using the microwave you will find it is a lot easier in many ways than your conventional cooker. It certainly stays cleaner and leaves less smells and dirt in your kitchen.

This cookery book has been designed to help you cook with your new microwave oven and is divided into different sections. The first few pages are a general introduction to microwave cookery; what containers you can use in the microwave oven at one time and all the basic guidelines you need to produce perfect results.

So, before you begin cooking, read this section carefully and thoroughly — then turn to the rest of the book. Recipe sections are divided into types of food i.e. poultry, meats, cakes. At the beginning of each chapter there are a few do's and don'ts to help you get the best results. Some of these recipes will be very new and some will be old favourites — but with the cooking method and timings altered. For these recipes, Toshiba has many people to thank as they have been tried and tested by microwave demonstrators throughout the country, my Micromag readers and, of course, Toshiba Home Economists. Each recipe will tell you the number of servings, how long it takes to cook and what cooking container to use. So read it carefully before starting. Happy microwaving!

Jay Oldknow, Home Appliance Adviser and Annemarie Rosier, Consultant Home Economist, testing recipes for the cookery book.

Introduction

The recipes have been written for 600 watt output ovens but timings have been included in boxes below each recipe to enable owners with different watt output ovens to use the book to the full.

500 watt output ovens with full power and defrost.
650 watt output ovens with full power and defrost.
650 watt output ovens with variable power.

Before each timing in the method of each recipe is a letter e.g. [a] 2 mins, the letter corresponds to the timings in the boxes below each recipe.

If you have a 500 watt output oven follow the timings under the 500 watt heading.

If you have a 650 watt output oven with full power and defrost follow the timings under the 650 watt/2 power

If you have a 650 watt ouput oven with variable power follow the timing under the 650 watt heading, e.g. if the method of a recipe says cook in the microwave oven for [a] 4 mins add the sugar and cook for a further [b] 3 mins. Stand for 5 mins before serving.

500 watt		650 watt /2 power	
a	5 mins	a	3½ mins
b	3 mins	b	2½ mins
650 watt			
a	PL.8 for 4 mins		
b	PL.9 for 1½ mins		

For a 500 watt ouput oven with full power and defrost you would — cook in the microwave oven for [a] 5 mins, add sugar and cook for a further [b] 3 mins. Stand for 5 mins before serving. Always use full power unless otherwise stated.

For a 650 watt output oven with full power and defrost, you would — cook in the microwave oven for [a] 3½ mins, add the sugar and cook for a further [b] 2½ mins. Stand for 5 mins before serving. Always use full power unless otherwise stated.

For a 650 watt output oven with variable power you would — cook in the microwave oven [a] Power Level 8 for 4 mins, add the sugar and cook for a further [b] PL.9 for 1½ mins. Stand for 5 mins before serving. When using a 650 watt output oven with variable power, many recipes suggest using a lower power level to obtain better results, when this happens the cooking time will have to be increased.

Back To Basics

Microwave ovens are very different from conventional cookers. It is essential you know how and why your oven works. Once the basics are understood, cooking,

defrosting and reheating will easily follow.

A microwave oven allows for cool, fast and inexpensive preparation of meals.

So what is a microwave?

A microwave is a short wave〜〜〜rather like a radio wave but shorter.

A microwave is reflected by metal:

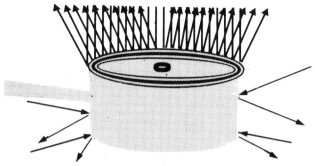

A microwave is transmitted or passes through china, glass, paper and Pyrex without heating it:

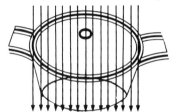

A microwave is absorbed by water molecules:

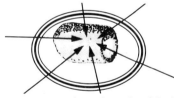

The microwaves produce heat by friction caused by moisture molecules in the food vibrating against each other very quickly. This is the same friction heat you experience when you rub your hands together on a cold day to warm them.

The microwaves penetrate into the food at the rate of 2450 million per second and for 1½″ into the food from the outside in.

If the food is thicker than 3″, the centre will cook by conduction of heat rather than by direct microwave action:

To sum up: microwaves penetrate food creating quick heat, but they will not directly heat the oven cavity or the container the food is in. This makes for economic, fast cooking.

Some foods microwave superbly and, once tried in the oven, you will never again want to use your conventional cooker for them. Some of these foods include:

Vegetables — always crisp and bright in colour.

Baked Potatoes — fluffy and moist.

Leftovers — always reheat without that "reheated" taste.

Scrambled eggs — greater volume.

Fish — moist and fresh tasting.

Bacon — clean cooking, good flavour.

Poultry — tender, moist and juicy.

Hot snacks — microwaved in minutes without fuss.

Some foods do not microwave well and these include:

Eggs in shells — they will burst.

Pancakes — reheat only.

Yorkshire Pudding — reheat only.

Large food loads such as a 20 lb turkey, or a dozen or more baked potatoes are more efficiently done in your conventional oven.

Just as with a conventional cooker, where various techniques are used, the same applies to microwave cooking. Some techniques are applicable to both forms of cooking — others are unique to microwave.

Cooking Techniques

Stirring — foods cooked or heated conventionally in a saucepan need a lot of stirring, but when done in the microwave oven less stirring is required. Scrambled eggs, sauces, custards, baked beans will need a stir once or twice only during the cooking cycle.

Stirring scrambled egg

Turning Over — When using a browning skillet, food must be turned over. The same procedure should be followed when cooking joints of meat or turkey. Items such as jacket potatoes also cook better if turned over halfway through the cooking cycle.

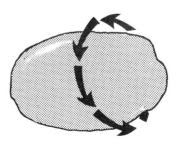

Standing Time — The most important phase in microwave cooking. In conventional cooking, roasts are left to stand before carving or cakes before turning out. With microwave cooking this is extended to cover all foods. When foods come out of the oven, they require standing time to finish cooking. This is because the microwaves create heat in the outer layers of the food which, during standing, is conducted into the centre, thus finishing the cooking process. The food will not lose heat rapidly during standing time, in fact, it gains in temperature for a time.

For example, a joint cooked to a temperature of 150°F/65°C in the oven will have reached a temperature of 165°F/75°C some 20 minutes after the microwave has been switched off and it will be ready to eat.

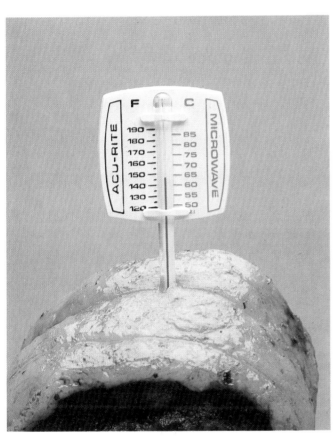

Temperature before standing time

Temperature after standing time

Rotating — Food should be rotated just as often in a microwave oven as in a conventional cooker. This is generally done for you by automatic turntable but if your model does not have an automatic turntable then you just turn the dish by hand once or twice during the cooking cycle.

Note: If the cooking container or item of food does not allow the automatic turntable to revolve, remove spindle and place dish on turntable or tray on the base of the oven. Food should then be turned by hand as required.

Covering — Covering of foods in both forms of cooking helps speed up the heating process and holds in moisture. With the microwave oven, a large selection of foods are covered for this reason.

Shielding of vulnerable areas

Pricking egg membrane

Shielding — When cooking in a conventional oven, some parts of certain foods often require shielding to prevent over-cooking or over-colouring. The same applies with a microwave oven. When cooking a turkey you will find that the breast, the edge of the wing and the edges of the leg will need to be wrapped in foil to prevent over-cooking. Use only very thin strips of foil and make sure that these pieces of foil are not touching the sides of the oven. As the amount of foil is so little and the amount of meat is so great by comparison, you will not harm the oven. This can also be done when you are defrosting or cooking large fish.

Pricking — Pricking foods is a technique used frequently in microwave cookery. When cooking a jacket potato, poached eggs or baked apples; the foods will need to be pricked before cooking. Food should never be cooked in a completely sealed container, such as a plastic bag. Always make sure that the bag is pricked so that steam can escape, otherwise the food inside the bag will try to burst out, making a mess in the oven.

Arrangement of food for the microwave oven

Arranging In A Dish — Always arrange foods with the thickest parts towards the outside of the dish. Foods of equal size such as jacket potatoes or stuffed tomatoes should be arranged in a circle in the microwave oven with the centre left clear. They will cook far more evenly this way. The same applies to small individual sponge cakes or when reheating more than one item.

10

Microwave Cooking Basics

The basics of microwave cooking are very similar to conventional cooking and just as with recipes in a conventional oven all timings are approximate, the same applies to the microwave oven. All the recipes have been checked against the different wattage outputs but each individual oven has its own characteristics so as with a conventional oven check the dish at the end of cooking time and adjust as required.

Length of Cooking Time — Learning how long to cook food is easy once you have become familiar with the various factors that influence cooking times. These are:

A **The amount of food that goes into the microwave oven.** When food is placed in the oven all the energy that comes into the microwave oven is absorbed into that one item of food. So as soon as you put more than one item into the oven, the waves have to be shared around. Consequently, the more food you put into the oven the longer it will take to heat. When placing more than one item in the oven, increase the time as follows:

If one food item takes 1 minute, then to cook two you have to add 50% additional time. For two it will take 1½ minutes, three will take 2 minutes. One plated meal will take you 2½ minutes in the microwave oven, two will take you 4½ minutes (always take the timing up to the nearest round figure for easier calculation).

B **Density.** The density of food determines how easily microwaves can penetrate and how quickly an item will cook. The more porous the food, the faster it will cook. For example, bread will cook much quicker than a meat burger.

C **Content.** Foods with a high fat or sugar content cook and reheat quicker in the oven. Foods with a high moisture content take longer. Therefore when cooking items such as cakes (high fat, high sugar, low moisture), be sure not to over cook. The same applies to heating jam tarts and other high sugar/fat foods.

D **Starting Temperature.** Just as with conventional cooking where the colder the food, the longer it will take to cook, so the same applies with the microwave oven. Food taken from the refrigerator or freezer will take longer to cook than if it is at room temperature.

E **Size and shape of food.** These two considerations also affect the timing. The smaller the food the faster it will cook. Thinner pieces will cook faster than thicker pieces. Round shaped items will cook faster than a square or oblong shape.

Fast or Slow in the Microwave Oven — Your microwave oven has a minimum of two power levels, probably called 'defrost' and 'cook'. Besides the lower power levels being used for defrosting, they can also be used for cooking and reheating of foods. Where you have nine different power levels on your microwave oven, then all of these can be used in combination with one another for the various functions the oven will perform. Some foods require slower cooking than others. Just as with conventional cooking, some foods will toughen if cooked too quickly or will dry out. The same can apply to microwave cooking. When using cheaper cuts of meat, cook on defrost or simmer. If cooking something you think might curdle or toughen, cook on a lower power level. The faster the speed at which the food is cooked the more attention it will need.

Food ready for reheating

Temperature Controlled Microwave Cooking

Certain models of microwave ovens now incorporate a Temperature Probe. This feature enables you to control the internal temperature of a food item and in fact take some of the "guesswork" or "testing" out of microwave cooking.

The probe is plugged into the socket provided in the cavity of the oven. It's metal tip is then placed into the food to be cooked or heated. Note: As long as the metal tip is inserted into food while the oven is working, it will not damage the oven. Now the oven control is set to the required temperature and when the internal temperature of the food reaches that heat, the oven will switch off.

The temperature probe can be combined with the power level, the Heat and Hold control or the Memory feature during operation of the microwave oven.

Heating foods with the temperature probe

Most food items can be heated using the temperature probe (see page 34). Heating foods by this method is the most accurate. Generally foods are heated on PL.8. Where a food requires heating to serving temperature, the instructions at the end of the recipe will read:

Temp probe (a) 80°C PL.8 — saying that instead of using timings as suggested for (a) in the recipe, insert temperature probe, set at 80°C on power level 8, stand or stir food before serving.

Cooking with the temperature probe

Joints of meat. Instructions for this are given on page 66 in the Temperature Probe Cooking Chart.

Heat and Hold. The Heat and Hold function must be used in conjunction with the temperature probe. It is used to **maintain** the food at the desired internal temperature. During this operation the oven will operate on PL.9 (full power) until the pre-set temperature is reached. The oven magnetron will then switch off and not transmit any microwave energy unless the internal temperature drops. When this happens, the temperature probe sends a message to the magnetron to transmit enough energy (at full power) to bring the food back up to the required temperature.

By using the Heat and Hold function, food can be kept warm for a short period of time i.e. for a late arrival or while you are out. Remember to keep the food covered and that the Heat and Hold is not a timed programme, so you have to turn off the oven.

Casseroles or Slow Cooking

Several recipes in the cookery book suggest the use of the Heat and Hold function for long, slow cooking. The temperature is set at around 90°C — 95°C and this ensures no over-cooking (see page 67 for full instructions). The time suggested is the minimum required as you can cook for a few minutes or all day with this control.

The temperature probe should not be used in conjunction with frozen food items while they are still frozen as this could damage the probe.

When using the temperature probe make sure that it is inserted firmly into the socket. After use it should immediately be wiped clean and stored out of the oven in a safe place. Never leave the probe in the oven when not in use.

Browning with a microwave oven

Microwave energy cooks the food so quickly that very often fat and sugars within the food will not have time to caramelize and give a brown appearance. These foods will need additional colouring to enhance their appearance and there are various ways of achieving the right result when you are cooking by microwave alone.

There are various browning agents on the market which can be used either in liquid form, such as gravy browning, soy sauce, Worcestershire sauce, hot pepper sauce. Alternatively you can use the powder forms, such as chicken seasoning or seasoned coating mixes. These will add different flavours and colour to your food. You can also make up your own colouring agents by mixing different ingredients together such as sherry with soy sauce, mustard with honey and a pinch of gravy browning. Slices of meat cannot be seared or coloured by microwave energy alone, since heat is produced directly in the food. Microwave browning dishes are available which, once they have been pre-heated in the microwave oven, can be used for sealing and colouring small items such as hamburgers, steaks or chops. The browning dish has been designed especially for the microwave oven and should not be used in any other type of oven or on any hot plate or hob. There are various types of browning dishes, all have a special coating on the base. When it is placed into the microwave oven, the bottom of the dish will get hot by absorbing microwave energy. Food is then placed onto the surface of the dish and will be browned by contact. Food has to be turned over halfway through the cooking cycle so that the other side can also be coloured.

To achieve maximum results with this special type of dish, damp off with paper towelling any food that is to be cooked so that the meat is as dry as possible. Spread a little butter onto the meat if necessary and then, once the dish is heated, press the meat firmly onto the browning dish. Heat for half the cooking time and then turn over and heat on the other side. If you are adding oil or any type of fat to the dish, do so only after the dish has been heated and before adding any food. The browning dish has to be boosted in temperature between cooking several items. Do *not* preheat the browning dish longer than the manufacturer's recommendation. It is advisable to use oven gloves when removing the browning dish from the oven and place the dish on a heat resistant surface. The browning dish should be cleaned after use and if stubborn marks are left, use a non-abrasive cleaner.

Microwave Cooking Utensils

When buying containers for the microwave oven look out for dishes that are labelled "microwave oven safe" or "recommended for use in a microwave oven", and remember that dishes with lugs or handles on the side are easier to use.

If you are not sure about a container's suitability in the oven, test it in the following way:

Place the dish in the oven. Place ¼ pint cold water in Pyrex jug alongside the dish or standing in it. Time for one minute. Water should be warm and dish cold. If dish is hot, do not use in the oven.

Do not use in the microwave oven:
Metal pots and pans
Metal baking trays
Conventional oven thermometers
Foil trays
Foil lined boxes and baking trays
Plates with gold, silver or platinum paint or edging

Avoid using:
Melamine
Eckoware
Tupperware

**But the following can be used
for the different applications as noted:**

Paper towels, serviettes and doylies	*for absorbing moisture*
Paper plates and cups	*heating food and liquid only*
Plastic foam plates and cups	*defrosting only and bread product reheating (**Note:** distorts with high fat temperatures).*
Cling film	*use as a covering on dishes*
Boilable bags	*defrosting/cooking/heating*
Freezer bags/Film	*defrosting only*
Roast bags	*cooking meats*
Plastic designed for use in boiling water	*for some cooking, heating and defrosting, may distort from fat and discolour with baked beans etc.*
Oven glass i.e. Pyrex	*ideal for defrosting/cooking/ heating*
Glass ceramic i.e. Pyrosil	*ideal for defrosting/cooking/ heating*

China/porcelain	*generally fine for defrosting and heating but look out for gold and silver edges*	
Stoneware	*suitable for defrosting/cooking/heating*	
Pottery	*suitable for heating and cooking but avoid unglazed dishes and dishes half glazed. Use dish test.*	
Glass	*short term heating. Do not use crystal*	
Straw and wood	*ideal for short term heating*	
Ovenable board	*this new material is used to make semi-disposable dishes. Ideal for freezing, cooking and heating. Also in conventional oven up to 400°F.*	

* **Note:** Avoid fluffy paper and red serviettes as they stick to food.

Utensils suitable for use in the microwave oven

14

Utensils not suitable for use in the microwave oven

Correct Shape Cooking Containers for Good Results

Just as the shape of food can affect the cooking result, so can the cooking container. Microwaves reach the food from all sides and cook from the outside in, so by altering the shape of the container, the cooking results will be changed.

Ring shaped. Microwaves have access to all sides of the food. The 'slow to cook' centre is removed.

Round. Microwaves have equal access to all sides. Centre cooks more slowly.

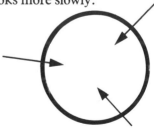

Square. Microwaves have double access to corners and over cooking can result.

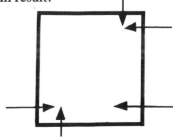

15

Oblong. Microwaves have double access to corners and on any large containers there is a slow to cook centre.

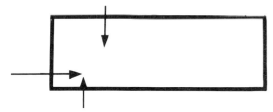

Straight sides/Flat base. Microwaves have equal access to top and bottom of food, but over cooking may occur at corners.

Slanted sides. Microwaves have double access to food at top edges

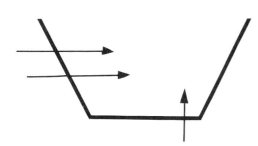

Straight sides/Round corners. Helps even out the microwave exposure by eliminating corners.

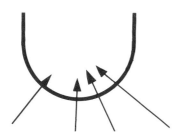

As you can see from the above diagrams, the dish shape is important to even cooking. When using dishes not so suitable for the oven, additional stirring and rearranging will be needed.

Covering food with cling film

Covering Hints

By covering food in the oven, moisture is retained in the dish and food. Covers also promote even heating and prevent splatters in the oven.

Type of food

Bacon, hot dog, sandwiches, jacket potatoes: Cover with paper towel or serviettes. The paper, being porous, lets the steam escape.

Stale bread rolls, fish fillets, pancakes: Cover with damp paper towels. These will help in the reheating.

Vegetables, casseroles: Cover utensil with lid or loose cling film.

Plated meals, corn on the cob: Cover lightly with cling film for maximum moisture retention.

Joints of meat, poultry items: Cover with a slit roasting bag.

Frozen food: Cover food lightly when defrosting except for cakes, bread and pies.

Do not cover during reheating fresh bread items, fruit or meat pies, pizzas or any food you wish to keep firm in the oven.

If you wish to dry food in the microwave oven i.e. herbs or breadcrumbs or freshen crisps, then place the food on absorbent paper.

Special Microwave Accessories

Plate Rings
Specially designed for the microwave oven to be used for stacking plates when reheating in the oven.

Microwave Oven Thermometers
These can go into the food when raw and stay in the oven throughout the cooking time.

Roasting Rack
A rack to hold the food out of the liquid which accumulates as meat cooks. Ideal for bacon and assists in reheating pastry and other dry items.

Cake Dishes
Bun rings designed to ensure even results when cooking cakes in a variety of shapes and sizes.

Hints & Helpful Tips

The microwave oven can be used for many things besides defrosting, reheating and cooking. It can be used to help in the preparation of foods and containers to use in cooking or in the serving of food items. For instance:

Drying Herbs

If you grow your own herbs, a microwave oven is ideal for the drying of these. Place a handful of picked herbs onto absorbent paper in the base of the oven ensuring the herbs are spread out. Heat gently, checking every 30 seconds until the herbs begin to dry. Do remember that the timing will vary with the type and amount of herb. Great care is needed if left too long in the oven they will tend to disintegrate and could ignite. Leave the herbs on the absorbent paper in a warm room for a couple of hours and then put into suitable containers.

Citrus Fruit

To make citrus fruit easier to peel, pop it into the microwave oven for just a few minutes i.e. one orange for about 25 seconds, six oranges or lemons for about 2 minutes. You will also find that the yield of fruit juice is greater after it has been prepared this way.

Skinning of Nuts & Fruit

Nuts and peaches can be skinned by heating in the microwave oven. Make a small slit in the peach skin. Place them in the oven and heat until just beginning to get warm and the skin will then slip off easily. Chestnuts also are easier to peel after they have been in the oven. Make small incision in the outer membrane and again, heat in the oven.

Refreshing Bread and Biscuits

For stale biscuits or crisps, pop them into the oven on absorbent paper and heat until warm. Leave to stand and they will have freshened up and be ideal to use. Bread can be freshened by the same method. If the bread is very stale, wrap it in a wet tissue. But *do* serve the bread within 20 minutes of heating.

Making Breadcrumbs

To make breadcrumbs or dry cubes of bread, grate the bread or chop it into cubes and then dry it in the oven on absorbent paper. Check every 30 seconds and gently shake paper to rearrange bread.

Dried Fruit

To save soaking dried fruit overnight, cover in boiling water, heat in the microwave oven for 5 minutes and allow to stand for an hour or so before using or cooking. If you want to plump up fruit for cakes, cover with water, bring to the boil in the oven, allow to stand for 3 minutes, drain and dry well.

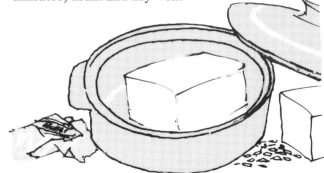

Softening Butter and Cheese

If you want to use butter straight from the fridge for a cake, or your cream cheese is too hard for spreading onto crackers, remove from foil or container, heat in the microwave oven for just a few seconds and you will find it easier to spread. Or, if cheese isn't quite ripe, such as Brie, pop it into the microwave oven for a few seconds to ripen just before you serve.

Blanching Potatoes

The microwave oven can also be used for blanching chips. If you are making your own chips or doing roast potatoes, peel and cut the potatoes into the required shapes. Place with a little water in a covered container, heat them in the microwave oven until warm, drain and then carry on to roast or fry in the conventional manner.

Browning Almonds

Almonds can be browned in the microwave oven. Place the almonds onto a Pyrex or heavy dish, spread out well and heat. Shake the dish every 1½ minutes, distributing the almonds until they are the required colour. Note that the dish will become hot.

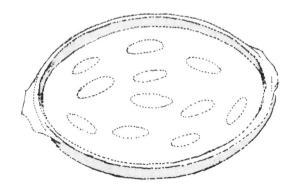

Chocolate

To melt chocolate in the microwave oven, break the chocolate into a suitable bowl, place into the microwave oven and heat for 1 minute at a time. Stir after every minute, when the chocolate is smooth remove from the oven. If the chocolate sets before it is required then return to the oven to be re-melted.

Marzipan

To soften marzipan and make it easier to knead, heat in the microwave oven for approximately 30 seconds on defrost or power level 3.

Cleaning Jam Jars

To get the last tablespoon out of a jam jar, honey jar or syrup jar, as long as the container is made of glass or plastic place it into the microwave oven and heat until the jam, honey or syrup is liquid. This will ensure that you will get the remains out of the jar.

Jelly Cubes

When making up an instant jelly mix break up the cubes of jelly and add ¼ pint cold water. Heat in the microwave oven until the jelly cubes are dissolved. Stir well and then top up to the required water level. Place the jelly into the refrigerator to set.

Adapting Your Favourite Recipes for use in the Microwave Oven

Each chapter in the book gives general guidelines on how to cook groups of food. Having read these carefully first, you will find some of the following significant differences compared with conventional cooking:

A **Ingredient changes** i.e. adding more or less moisture, adding less fat to the recipe.

B **Timing changes.** Conventionally, the dish may take 40 minutes to cook, by microwave it will probably take only 12 minutes.

C **The cooking container.** For conventional cookery, you may be using a saucepan, in the microwave oven it is probably a serving dish.

D **Arrangement in the dish.** Conventionally this doesn't usually matter but with microwave cooking you will get better results with proper arrangement of food.

In the first recipe below you will notice that there are no changes in the recipe ingredients but there are changes in the cooking method, the cooking container and the timing.

Apple Suet Pudding *(Conventional method)*

6 oz (175g) suet crust pastry
1 lb (450g) cooking apples, peeled, cored and sliced
4 oz (100g) granulated sugar)

Cooking container: 1½ pint basin/steamer
Cooking time: 2½ hours
Number of servings: 4-6

Half fill a steamer with water and put it on to boil. Grease a 1½ pint pudding basin. Make pastry and roll out. Use ¾ of the pastry to line the basin, fill the basin with sliced apples and sprinkle with the sugar in alternate layers. Use the remaining pastry to make a lid, damp the edges of the pastry in the basin and cover with lid, pressing the edges well together. Cover with greased greaseproof paper and steam for 2½ hours. Turn out the pudding when ready to serve.

Apple Suet Pudding *(Microwave method)*

6 oz (175g) suet crust pastry
1 lb (450g) cooking apples, peeled, cored and sliced
4 oz (100g) granulated sugar

Cooking container: 1½ pint bowl
Cooking time: 6 minutes
Number of servings: 4-6

Grease a 1½ pint pudding basin. Make the pastry and roll out. Line the bowl with ¾ of the pastry. Fill the bowl with the apples and sugar in alternate layers. Make a lid with the remaining pastry, damp the edges of the pastry in the basin and cover with a lid, pressing the edges well together. Cover with cling film, cook in the microwave oven for 6 minutes. Turn out when ready to serve.

It is not possible in the microwave oven to achieve exactly the same result as with conventional cooking always, but with this next recipe the flavour is just as good and the colouring very good indeed. In this recipe there are ingredient as well as time and container changes.

Pineapple With Gammon *(Conventional method)*

2 gammon rashers, cut ½" thick
8 oz (225g) can pineapple rings
2½ oz (37g) butter
4 level tablespoons (60 ml) demerara sugar

Cooking container: Frying pan
Cooking time: 35 minutes
Number of servings: 2-4

Trim the rashers and snip the fat at intervals. Cut each rasher in half, drain the pineapple rings retaining the juice. Poach the rashers in a little water for 1-2 minutes and throw away the water. Fry the rashers in the butter until golden brown on both sides. Remove rashers and cool the remaining butter. Add the pineapple juice and sugar, dissolve over a low heat and bring to the boil. Return the rashers to the pan, reduce the heat and cover and simmer for about 20 minutes until tender. Arrange the rashers onto a serving dish and reduce the liquor slightly by boiling. Add the pineapple rings and heat through. Arrange them on top of the rashers and pour glaze over them.

Pineapple With Gammon *(Microwave method)*

2 gammon rashers cut ½" thick
8 oz (225g) can pineapple rings
½ oz (12g) butter
4 level tablespoons (60 ml) demerara sugar

Cooking container: shallow dish
Cooking time: 14½ minutes
Serves 2-4

Trim the rashers and snip the fat at intervals. Cut each rasher in half. Drain the pineapple rings retaining the juice. Place the gammon rashers onto absorbent paper or onto a roasting rack. Cook in the microwave oven for 4 minutes. Drain off any juice, stand the gammon rashers to one side. Into a shallow dish place the sugar, butter and pineapple juice, heat in the microwave oven for 6 minutes, stirring well after 3 minutes and at the end of the cooking cycle. Add the gammon rashers to the juice and baste well with the liquid. Heat in the microwave oven for 3 minutes. Arrange the pineapple rings onto the gammon and heat for a further 1½ minutes.

When looking for recipes to convert to use in the microwave oven, look for those which use similar cooking techniques to microwave cooking techniques, such as covering, steaming, cooking in a sauce or in a liquid. If the food requires a crisp, fried crust or a very dry surface you may prefer to cook it conventionally. Some recipes may not be exactly the same when micro-waved but you will find the results are very good.

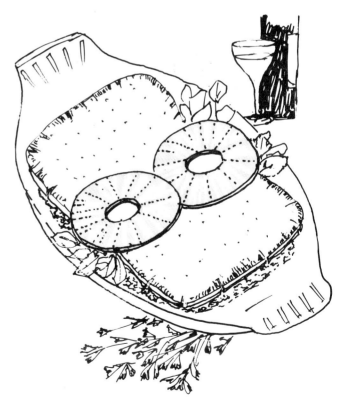

Combination Cooking

By using your microwave oven in conjunction with conventional equipment already in your kitchen, you will be able to achieve lots of different finishes and flavours to the food. This way you will not only get better use out of your microwave oven but also better use out of your conventional equipment, including the freezer.

Microwave Oven and The Conventional Oven

For instance, the oven of your conventional cooker can be used for the cooking of pastry items to give a better colour result than in the microwave oven, so why not batch bake fruit pies and meat pies, freeze them down and then defrost and reheat as required. If you are making bread, use the microwave oven for proving the dough and finish off the baking in the conventional cooker (brown bread can be done very satisfactorily in the microwave oven, but for white bread and white rolls you may prefer the finish that the conventional oven gives you). For roast potatoes, pre-blanch the potatoes in the microwave oven with just a small amount of water and then pop them into the conventional oven in a little oil. Joints of meat needing a traditional crisp finish can be finished off in your conventional cooker. Do this instead of leaving them outside the microwave oven as part of their standing time.

Microwave Oven and The Grill

A microwave oven used in combination with a grill will give you the best of both worlds. Portions of meat such as chicken, steaks, pork or lamb chops and sausages can be popped under the grill, quickly coloured and then placed into the microwave oven to finish, which makes sure the meat is not dried out, as sometimes happens with grilling. The result is a dish with the brown appearance you require, but with a juicy flavour achieved only by microwave cooking.

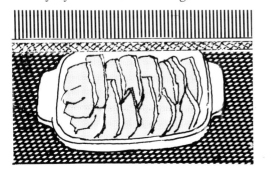

For dishes such as cauliflower cheese or lasagne, or any dish which requires a brown topping, it only takes a few seconds to heat up the grill just to colour the dish.

Microwave Oven and The Hob

The microwave oven and the hob is also a useful combination. Firstly, to seal meat and vegetables in a frying pan before turning it onto a different dish for a microwave oven casserole. A frying pan is ideal too for colouring chicken and duck portions to be used in a casserole.

Microwave Oven and The Kettle

The electric kettle in the kitchen is also a valuable asset to save time when cooking pasta items, packet soups and suchlike. Bring the water to the boil in the kettle and then add to the soup and finish cooking in the microwave oven.

Microwave Oven and The Toaster

Toasted sandwiches can be so easy. After toasting the bread, cheese slices can be placed on to the toast and then heated in the microwave. The same system can be used for crumpets. Toast them in advance and then just heat them in the microwave as required.

Microwave Oven and The Freezer

The most obvious and elementary partnership of all. Whenever you are making soups or sauces, or in fact any meal, always try to make double the quantity and freeze the other half, defrosting and reheating when required. With plated meals, any food leftovers can be frozen down on paper, china or Pyrex plates. Cover with freezer film once the food is cold before you freeze. At a later date just take out the plates and heat. You will soon find you can get better use of your freezer. The freezer no longer becomes a store cupboard with you wondering what is at the bottom of it. You will always be using your freezer when you have a microwave oven.

Care of Your Microwave Oven — Your microwave oven will give you many years of carefree service as long as it is properly looked after. The oven should be kept clean. This is very easy as the walls of the oven never get hot, so food will not be baked onto the sides of the oven leaving those nasty stubborn black deposits. Clean the oven by wiping it out with a damp, soapy cloth. Pay special attention to cleaning the door and especially the door seals. These should always be kept free of any dirt. The oven base tray can be removed and cleaned in the sink or dishwasher. It is important that the tray and the interior of the oven is never cleaned with a wire wool pad, or an abrasive, as scratches can affect the performance of the microwave oven. Don't use soap pads on the outside of the door, either. If there are any stubborn marks in your microwave that are difficult to clean out, boil water inside the oven for a few minutes and the steam will loosen any dirt. The outside casing of the oven can be wiped over with a damp soapy cloth at regular intervals and polished lightly with a spray polish like any other item of equipment in the kitchen.

Note: If you have a disaster in your microwave oven like overheating a Christmas pudding and you tend to get a slight burnt smell, boil water and lemon in the microwave for about 10 minutes and repeat this at regular intervals, two or three times a week. This will get rid of the smell. If your oven stops working for any reason, first check that the fuse in the plug has not blown before calling for a service engineer.

The right way to clean your microwave oven

The wrong way to clean your microwave oven

Meal Planning

Once you have used your microwave oven for a variety of dishes you will be ready to start cooking complete meals.

Below are guidelines to preparing a complete meal in the microwave oven:-

The idea is to prepare and cook the food so that everything is ready to serve at the same time.

Before you start cooking:-
1 Plan the menu.
2 Read the recipes and have all the ingredients and utensils ready.
3 Decide which dishes can be reheated rather than cooked and served straight-away.

4 Anything to be served cold should be cooked in advance.

The correct cooking order is decided by the heat retaining quality of the foods. Foods that retain heat longest are cooked first.

Cook first — meats, baked potatoes and casseroles.
Cook second — fish, vegetables, sauces and gravies.

Remember that if anything cools, it can be reheated before serving.

Puddings and custards can be cooked beforehand and reheated or cooked during eating of the main course.

Below are two sample menus to guide you.

Sunday Dinner

Number of servings: 4

Menu
Microwave roast pork
Roast potatoes
Stuffing
2 vegetables
Gravy
Apple sauce

Brandy Coffee Cake

Work order
1 Brandy coffee cake
2 Pork
3 Potatoes
4 Stuffing
5 Gravy
6 Vegetables

Work method
1 Prepare and cook coffee cake.
2 Prepare stuffing.
3 Cook pork in oven approximately 8 minutes to 1 lb. Leave to stand either in pre-heated oven or under grill.
4 Blanch potatoes for 6 minutes. Place in pre-heated oven or under grill with oil.
5 Cook stuffing.
6 Cook gravy.
7 Cook vegetables.
8 Reheat gravy and stuffing before serving.

Number of servings: 4

Menu
Tomato Soup
Spicy Meat Loaf
Jacket Potatoes
Green Salad
Pineapple Upside Down Pudding

Work order:
1 Soup
2 Meat Loaf
3 Potatoes
4 Soup (reheat)
5 Meat Loaf (finishing)
6 Sweet

Work method:
1 Prepare and cook soup.
2 Prepare and half cook meat loaf, add topping and leave to stand.
3 Cook potatoes and wrap in foil.
4 Heat soup and serve.
5 Finish cooking meat loaf while eating soup.
6 Cook sweet while eating main course.

Defrosting

Defrosting

Defrosting with the microwave oven ensures total cooking convenience and the freezer becomes no longer just another storage cupboard, but an integral part of your cooking system.

Once food has been defrosted it requires a standing time before being cooked or heated. This ensures all the ice crystals are melted and the end result will be an even temperature.

Food frozen yourself will generally take longer to defrost than commercially frozen food. This is due to larger ice crystals in the food.

Freeze food for the microwave oven in suitable containers as this saves turning out into another dish.

When freezing plated meals make sure that the meal is really cold before freezing and always freeze covered.

Microwave method for defrosting fish:-
Always cover fish during defrosting. Drain off all excess water from defrosted fish and dry with paper towel before cooking.

Microwave method for defrosting fruit:-
If fruit is in separate pieces, such as strawberries or plums, then spread out in container, defrost for the required time but rearrange the fruit during the defrosting time. Standing time is essential when defrosting fruit to make sure that no cooking starts before defrosting has finished. If fruit is in a syrup then break up block gently as soon as possible.

Microwave method for defrosting vegetables:-
Vegetables can be cooked straight through from the frozen state.

Microwave method for defrosting pasta:-
When defrosting frozen pasta or rice, separate during the defrosting time as quickly as possible. Always defrost covered. If defrosting a thick pasta item such as lasagne or cannelloni ensure adequate standing time is given before heating.

Microwave method for defrosting bread:-
Bread rolls — place onto absorbent paper to defrost.
Sliced bread — remove from bag and place onto absorbent paper.
Separate the slices into separate piles as soon as possible during defrosting.

Microwave method for defrosting pastry items:-
Remove from foil container if it is in one. Pies need a good standing time before reheating as the centre is often very solid. It helps to defrost pastry items on a roasting rack.

Microwave method for defrosting boil-in-the-bag items:-
Make a hole in the bag before defrosting. Shake the contents gently before heating.

Removing food in foil trays for defrosting

Microwave method for defrosting food in foil trays:-
Turn frozen food out of foil containers into a dish of approximately the same size and cover with cling film.

Microwave method for defrosting casseroles or liquids:-
Casseroles or liquids should be stirred and broken up as soon as possible during defrosting. Keep covered.

Microwave method for defrosting plated meals:-
Defrost covered.

Microwave method for defrosting joints and poultry:-
Defrost covered; turn over once during defrosting.
Cover legs or thin ends with foil strips. Standing time is
essential before cooking.

Microwave method for defrosting meat:-
Separate solid blocks of meat e.g. mince as soon as
possible. Defrost covered.

Separating meat during defrosting

Microwave method for defrosting butter:-
Remove butter from foil wrap. Place onto dish and
defrost uncovered.

Microwave method for defrosting raw pastry:-
Remove pastry from foil wrap. Wrap loosely with
kitchen paper.

Microwave method for defrosting cakes and pastries:
Pastries — Place onto roasting rack or kitchen paper —
do not cover.

**Microwave method for defrosting single convenience
sweets i.e. Yoghurt, Mousse etc:-**
Remove lid before defrosting.

Freezer/Microwave Oven tips:-
1 Keep a supply of sweet and savoury pre-cooked flan
  cases in the freezer. Quiches and fruit flans can be
  made in minutes. Pancakes are another good
  standby.
2 Freeze pies in a cooked state rather than raw for
  quick serving.
3 A supply of frozen cooked pasta and rice is always
  useful.
4 Cook an extra portion of Sunday lunch and freeze it
  down for later use.

Defrosting Chart

Timings in this chart are approximate because freezer temperatures and methods vary. If the food is not completely thawed after standing, return to the oven for a short additional time and allow to stand. Always use the defrost level when defrosting.

Variable Power Oven

When defrosting food with the variable power oven, use power level 3 and follow the chart below for items weighing under 3 lb. Use the two power level charts for larger items.

Approx. Defrosting and Standing time (mins)

Food Item	Weight	500 watt	600 watt	650 watt/ 2 power	650 watt/ PL.3	Standing time
Convenience Foods						
Plated meal	12 oz.	5	3½	4	4	5
Plated meal	16 oz.	7½	6½	6½	6½	5
6 frozen pancakes		3	2	2	2	2
½ pint frozen sauce		8	7	7	7	5
1 pint thick soup		18	15	15	15	10
1 pint thin soup		15	11	12	12	10
1 family size pizza		5	4	3½	3½	5
1 individual lasagne		8	7	7	7	10
1 individual cannelloni		6	5½	5½	5½	10
Faggots in gravy		8	6	6	6	10
Lasagne	1 lb.	16	14	15	15	10
4" pizza		2½	1½	1½	1½	3
Paella		3½	2½	2½	2½	20
Meat/Poultry						
Timings given per lb. unless otherwise stated						
Mince	1 lb.	10	8	9	9	10
Bacon	8 oz.	3½	3	3	3	5
Sausages	1 lb.	7	6½	6	6	5
Liver	1 lb.	9	8½	8	8	5
Stewing Steak	1 lb.	11	10	10	10	10
Turkey roll	2 lb.	6	5	6	6	30
Lamb joint		12	8	8-10	8-10	20
Beef joint		12	8½	8-10	8-10	20
Pork joint		12	9	8-10	8-10	20
Lamb or pork chops	1 lb.	9	7	6	6	15
Shepherds pie	1 lb.	10	8	8	8	10
Steaks	2 x 6 oz.	8	8	7½	7½	10
Chicken portions	1 lb.	12	10	10	10	10
Chicken		12	8	9	9	10

continued on page 30, 31

A selection of food suitable for defrosting P.29

Food Item	Weight	500 watt	600 watt	650 watt/ 2 power	650 watt/ PL.3	Standing time
Casseroles						
Poultry in sauce	9 oz.	8	6½	7	7	5
6 portion chicken casserole		45	40	40	40	20
Beef casserole for 4		25	24	25	25	20
Fish						
Prawns	8 oz	4½	4	4	4	5
Haddock fillets	8 oz.	4	3	4	4	3
Kipper fillets	14 oz	5	4	5	5	3
Trout	1 lb.	12	9½	9	9	10
Dover Sole	11 oz.	7½	6½	7	7	5
Plaice fillets	1 lb.	9	8	4	4	5
4 cod steaks	4 x 3½ oz.	7	7	6	6	5
Boil-in-the-bag Fish in sauce	5 oz.	3½	4	5	5	3
Boil-in-the-bag Prawn curry	6 oz.	6½	5½	5½	5½	2
Fish casserole for 4		18½	16½	16½	16½	10
Prawns	4 oz.	3½	2½	2½	2½	2
Trout	7 oz.	6	4½	4¾	4¾	2
Fruit						
Raspberries	12 oz.	5	4½	5	5	10
Apples	1 lb.	6	5	4½	4½	10
Strawberries	1 lb.	6	4	4	4	10
Melon balls	1 lb.	6	4	4	4	10
Puddings/Cakes						
1 doughnut		45 secs.	45 secs.	30 secs.	30 secs.	5
6 scones		2½	2	3	3	10
Family size sponge cake		3	2	2½	2½	10
Family size cream sponge cake		1½	1½	1½	1½	20
1 individual mousse		1	30 secs.	45 secs.	45 secs.	15
1 individual trifle		1½	1	1	1	15
1 family size cheese cake		3	2½	3	3	20
1 family size fruit crumble		15	14	13	13	20

Food Item	Weight	500 watt	600 watt	650 watt/ 2 power	650 watt/ PL.3	Standing time
Pastry						
Savoury flan	9 oz.	6	5	5	5	5
1 Danish pastry		45 secs.	45 secs.	45 secs.	45 secs.	5
1 apple strudel		1	30 secs.	30 secs.	30 secs.	5
1 individual fruit pie		1½	1	1½	1½	5
1 family fruit pie 9"		11	10	10	10	10
Pastry	8 oz.	1½	1	1	1	15
Pastry	14 oz.	2½	2	2	2	20
Meat pie	5 oz.	3	2½	2½	2½	5
Family size meat pie 6"		7	7	6½	6½	10
Family size quiche 6"		5	4	5	5	5
Miscellaneous						
Large sliced loaf		9	7	8	8	10
6 croissants		2½	1½	1½	1½	3
1 bread roll		1	1	1	1	2
4 bread rolls		2	2	2	2	5
1 pint frozen sauce		14	13	13	13	15

The timings above are approximate and depend on the size, shape, weight and starting temperatures of the food. This chart is only a guideline, if defrosting is not complete after standing time, return to the oven for a few more minutes.

Two Power-Level Defrosting

Use two power levels when defrosting larger items i.e. joints over 3 lb in weight as they are more evenly and quickly defrosted. Turn food over halfway through defrosting. Remember to allow for standing time and if food has to be returned to the oven use the lower power level.

Food Item	Time PL.5 mins per lb	Time PL.2 mins per lb	Standing time mins per lb
Chicken	2	8	20
Duck	2	8	20
Pork boned and rolled	2	8	30
Pork with bone	2	8	30
Lamb	2	8	30
Turkey	3	7	20
Beef	2	8	30
Capon	3	7	20

Reheating

Reheating

The microwave oven is ideal for reheating foods. You will find you do not lose any flavour, colour, vitamin content or moisture when you reheat this way. Meals can be prepared in advance and heated by any member of the family and because the oven reheats so well, you will find you will incur less wastage.

Microwave method:

Canned Food Items

1 Open can and place contents onto a suitable serving dish.
2 For one portion of baked beans, spoon straight onto a slice of toast on the serving plate.
3 Cover where directed in the heating chart and heat for the required amount of time.

Canned food

Pastry Items

Pastry products should either be heated on kitchen paper or on a roasting rack. This ensures they will not come out of the microwave oven damp. If the centre of the pastry has a high fat or high sugar content, remember that the filling will heat quicker so be careful when heating jam tarts or the jam may tend to overheat. Do not cover pastry items in the microwave oven.

Plated Meals

When plating a meal make sure the food is as even in height as possible. Thicker items should be placed to the sides of the plate but all foods should be placed within the well of the plate. Cover with another plate or cling film and heat for the required time. Plates can be stacked in the microwave oven by using plate stackers. Never place the plates more than 2 high, cover the top plate and remember to increase the heating time by 50%.

Plated meals

Liquids

When heating liquids for sauces, gravy and custards, remember to stir halfway through the heating time and also on removal from the oven.

Casseroles

33

Bread Products

Heat bread rolls on absorbent paper, uncovered.

Pizzas, Quiches, Flans etc

Heat on absorbent paper or on a roasting rack. Pizzas can also be heated on a browning dish. Do not cover to reheat.

Pasta Dishes

Heat out of foil in serving dish, covered. Large items can be helped by heating on a combination of defrost and full power.

Baby Foods

Baby foods and drinks can be heated in the oven in the serving container. This includes drinks in a bottle. Baby foods should be stirred before serving.

Baby foods

Casseroles

Casseroles should be heated covered and stirred halfway through the heating time. Re-cover the casserole and carry on heating. Stir on removal from the oven and allow to stand for a couple of minutes before serving.

Slices of meat or small meat portions

When reheating slices of meat always add a small amount of meat juices or gravy to the meat. Cover and reheat for the required time. Overheating of meat may tend to toughen it.

Christmas Pudding

Christmas puddings can be reheated very successfully in the microwave oven but it is important they are carefully timed. If the pudding is heated for too long, the inside which has a high fat and sugar content could ignite, so follow the guidelines for reheating carefully. It is preferable to reheat Christmas pudding on a plate rather than in a plastic bowl.

Reheating with the temperature probe

Most foods can be heated in the microwave oven using the temperature probe. It is important to follow the general guidelines as mentioned in the last two pages.

Method: Connect the probe into the oven socket and insert the probe into the centre or thickest part of the food to be heated. So food items such as:
Drinks, Sauces, Soups, Custards, Casseroles, Baked beans, Milk puddings etc — insert probe into centre of the liquid and stir food before serving.

Food items such as:
Joints of meat, Poultry, meat and fruit pies, Christmas pudding and plated meals — insert probe into thickest part of item. Avoid touching bone or fat as these heat to a different temperature.

Use the temperature settings mentioned in the heating chart as a guideline to personal preference. Stand foods before serving.

A selection of food suitable for reheating P.35

34

Reheating Chart (time in mins)

Item	500 watt	600 watt	650 watt/ 2 power	650 watt/ PL.8	Temp. Probe	Standing time
Convenience Foods						
1 large lasagne	17	15	13	15	80°C-85°C	10
1 large cannelloni	15½	12	10	12	80°C-85°C	10
single portion lasagne	4½	3½	3	3½	80°C-85°C	2
1 single portion cannelloni	3	2½	2½	3	80°C-85°C	2
1 x 12oz. plated meal	4	3½	3-3½	3½	80°C-85°C	3
1 x 16oz. plated meal	5	4	3½-4	4	80°C-85°C	3
1 can cook-in-sauce	4	3½	3½	3½	75°C	2
1 x 7fl. oz. bowl thick soup	2½	3	2½	3	80°C	2
1 x 7fl. oz. bowl thin soup	2½	2½	2	2½	75°C-80°C	2
1½ pints thick soup	8½	8	8	8	75°C-80°C	5
1½ pints thin soup	9	6	6	6	75°C	5
4 oz. baked beans	2	1½	1	1½	90°C	2
8 oz. baked beans	3½	3	2½	3	90°C	2
16 oz. baked beans	6-7	6	5	6	85°C	3
Single portion ravioli	4	3½	2½-3	3½	85°C-90°C	2
Single portion macaroni cheese	3½	2	2-2½	2	85°C	2
Family sized macaroni cheese	10-11	9	8-10	9	85°C	5
4″ Pizza	2½	2	1½	2		2
Meats/Poultry						
Chicken portion 9 oz.	3½	2½	2	2½		3
4 x chicken portion	10	8	6-7	8		5
1 x 6 oz. steak	1½	1	45 secs-1 min	1		3
4 x 6 oz. steak	4	3	3	3		5
Portion sliced beef with gravy	2½	1½	1	1½		2
4 portions sliced beef with gravy	7-7½	6	4½	6		3
4 oz. bacon	4½	3½	3	3½		2
1 meat loaf	7½	7	6-7	7		5
8 oz. chops	2½-3	2	2	2		3
1lb. chops	4-5	3	3	3		5
1lb. liver	3½	2½	2	2½		5
1lb. sausages	6	4½	4	4½		5
4 x 2 oz. hamburgers	2½	1½	1½	1½		2
Fish						
1 x 7 oz. trout	2	1½	1	1½		2
1lb. cod	4	2½	2½	2½		4
8 oz. kipper fillets	2	1½	1½	1½		2
12 oz. haddock fillets	3	2	2	2		2
1 cod steak	1	1½	1	1½		2
4 cod steaks in sauce	3	2½	2½	2½		5
4 portion casserole of fish	12-14	10-12	8-10	10-12	85°C-90°C	5
1 portion fish fingers	1½	1	45 secs	1		2
4 portions fish fingers	3-3½	2½	2	2½		3

Item	500 watt	600 watt	650 watt/ 2 power	650 watt/ PL.8	Temp. Probe	Standing time
Casseroles						
Portion of chicken and mushroom casserole	3	2	1½-2	2	80°C-85°C	3
Family size mice beef casserole	15	12	12	12	80°C-85°C	5
6 portion chicken casserole	21	17	15	17	80°C-85°C	5
4 portion beef casserole	15	14	13	14	80°C-85°C	5
Vegetables						
4 oz. vegetables	1	45 secs.	30 secs.	30 secs.		2
9 oz. vegetables	1½	1	1	1		2
1lb. vegetables	3	2½	2½	2½	80°C-85°C	5
Pudding/Cakes						
Mini Christmas pudding	2	1½	1	1¼		3
1½lb. Christmas pudding	5	3½	3	3½		5
Whole sponge pudding	3	2	2	2		5
Portion sponge pudding	1	1	30 secs.	45 secs.		3
lb. stewed fruit	6	4½	4	4½	75°C-80°C	5
Baked apple 10 oz.	2	1½	1	1½	75°C-80°C	3
1 family sized fruit crumble	7	5½	5	5½	75°C-80°C	5
Pastry						
1 x family meat pie	4	4½	3-4	4½		5
1 single meat pie	2	1	45 secs.	1	80°C-85°C	2
1 single quiche	2	1	45 secs.	1		2
1 family size quiche	6-7	5	3-4	5		3
Treacle flan	2	1½	1¼	1½		3
1 individual fruit pie	1	1	30 secs.	45 secs.	75°C-80°C	2
1 family size fruit pie	2	1½	1½	1½		2
1 portion fruit pie and custard	1	1	30-45 secs.	45 secs.		2
6 individual mince pies	1½	1	45 secs-1 min 1			4
Miscellaneous						
1 can baby food	1½	1	1	1	50°C	2
Pancakes x 2 flat	1	1	30 secs.	45 secs.		2
Pancakes x 6 stuffed	3	2½	2	2½		3
1 pint custard	4½	4	3½	4	80°C	3
4 bread rolls	1	1	30 secs.	45 secs.		3
6 scones	1½	1	45 secs-1 min 1			4
½ pint thin sauce	3	2	2	2	80°C-85°C	4
1 pint thick sauce	3	2	2	2	80°C	4
Family size rice pudding	8	6	5	6	80°C	5

The timings above are approximate and depend on the size, shape, weight and starting temperatures of the food. This chart is only a guideline and if after standing time, the food is still not hot enough, return for another minute or two depending on the size of the food.

Snacks and Savouries

Snacks and Savouries

Whether it is beans on toast or your favourite appetizer, food can be heated by the oven in minutes. For parties, you have no need to be stuck in a hot kitchen producing the snacks. Your microwave oven and food can be taken into the room where it is going to be served and guests can almost heat their own.

As a general rule:

1 Cook covered any dips, appetizers or sauces.
2 Uncover any items such as bread or crackers as these could become very moist when heated.
3 Place a paper doily, serviette or absorbent paper under pastry and biscuits when reheating as this will help absorb any moisture.

Microwave method:

1 When reheating single items or snacks such as canapes, place them into a circle on a dish and this way they will reheat evenly.
2 When reheating a quantity of baked beans you may find it easier to heat the beans in a large bowl stirring once or twice during the heating cycle and then just pop in the toast for a few seconds before serving.

Beefburgers

Beef Burgers

Cooking container: Roasting rack
Cooking time: 6½ minutes
Number of servings: 4

4 x ¼ lb (100 g) burgers defrosted
4 baps
pepper
salt
garlic seasoning (optional)

Place the defrosted burgers onto a roasting rack. Sprinkle with a little seasoning and cook in the oven. The burgers can be brushed with soy sauce or gravy browning to give a darker colour but as they are to be served inside a bun it is not really necessary for the burgers to be a deep brown. Cook for [a] 6 minutes. Remove burgers from oven and allow to stand. Heat the baps in the oven for [b] 30 seconds, place the burgers into the baps and add any relishes or salad as required and serve. If using canned hamburgers, then place the hamburger inside a bread roll. Cheese or other flavourings can be added at this point. Heat on absorbent paper for approximately [c] 45 seconds for one burger and approximately [d] 2½ minutes for four burgers.

	500 watt		650 watt/2 power
a	7½ minutes	a	5 minutes
b	30 seconds	b	30 seconds
c	45 seconds	c	45 seconds
d	3½ minutes	d	2½ minutes

	650 watt
a	PL.7 for 6½ minutes
b	PL.9 for 30 seconds
c	PL.9 for 1 minutes
d	P.9 for 2½ minutes

Bacon wrapped Frankfurters

See colour plate page 41

Cooking container: Roasting Rack
Cooking time: 5 minutes
Number of servings: 20

10 rashers streaky bacon
10 frankfurter sausages

Cut the frankfurters in half. Remove rind and any bones from the bacon, cut in half and stretch. Wrap the bacon around the frankfurters and place onto a roasting rack. Cook 10 at a time for [a] 5 minutes.

	500 watt		650 watt/2 power
a	7 minutes	a	4½ minutes

	650 watt
a	PL.8 for 4 minutes

Beef Cheeseburgers

Cooking container: Roasting rack
Cooking time: 8-10 minutes
Number of servings: 4

1 lb (450 g) minced beef
1 onion, peeled and grated
2 oz. (50 g) grated cheese
4 tablespoons (60 ml) crushed breakfast cereal
few drops Worcestershire Sauce
salt and pepper

Combine all ingredients and form into 4 burgers. Place onto roasting rack and cook for [a] 8-10 minutes. Serve in baps.

500 watt		650 watt/2 power	
a	12-14 minutes	a	6-8 minutes
650 watt			
a	PL.7 for 10-12 minutes		

Peanut Burgers

Cooking container: Browning dish
Cooking time: 3 to 5 minutes according to taste
Number of servings: 4

1 lb (450 g) good quality minced beef
2 oz. (50 g) lightly crushed peanuts
salt and pepper

Mix meat with peanuts and seasoning to taste. Form into four burgers and set in the refrigerator for 30 minutes. Heat the browning dish for [a] 6 minutes. Press the burgers onto the base of the skillet. Cook for [b] 2 minutes. Drain off surplus fat, turn the burgers. Cook for a further [c] minute for rare, [c] 1½ minutes for medium and [c] 2 minutes for well done.

Suitable for freezing.

500 watt		650 watt/2 power	
a	7 minutes	a	6 minutes
b	3 minutes	b	2 minutes
c	3-4 mintues	c	1, 1½ or 2 minutes
650 watt			
a	PL.8 for 5½ minutes		
b	PL. 8 for 2 minutes		
c	PL.8 for 1, 1½ or 2 minutes		

Savoury Pancakes

Cooking container: Shallow serving dish
Cooking time: 11 minutes
Number of servings: 4

8 frozen pancakes
10½ oz. (298 g) can condensed cream of chicken soup, undiluted
8 oz. (225 g) chicken, chopped
4 oz. (100 g) prawns, canned, frozen or fresh
salt and pepper
3 tablespoons (45 ml) milk or white wine

Mix the prawns and chicken with half the condensed soup. Heat for [a] 2 minutes in the oven and check for seasoning. Divide the filling between the pancakes and roll up the pancakes around the filling. Place onto shallow serving dish. Mix the wine or milk with the rest of the soup and heat in the microwave oven for [b] 1 minute. Pour this over the pancakes and return to the oven for [c] 8 minutes. Serve hot.

This filling can be varied by using different condensed soups or, of course, your own sauce recipe. Any left over meat or vegetables can be added to the sauce. Pancakes can be stuffed and then frozen.

500 watt		650 watt/2 power	
a	3 minutes	a	1¾ minutes
b	2 minutes	b	1 minute
c	9-10 minutes	c	6 minutes
650 watt			
a	PL.8 for 2 minutes		
b	P.8 for 1 minute		
c	PL.8 for 7½ minutes		

Baked Beans on Toast

Cooking container: Serving plate
Cooking time: 2 minutes
Number of servings: 1

1 x 7¾ oz. tin baked beans
1 slice buttered toast

Place toast on serving plate, top with baked beans and heat for [a] 2 minutes.

500 watt		650 watt/2 power	
a	2½-3 minutes	a	2 minutes
650 watt			
a	PL.8 for 2 minutes		

Crab Canapes

Cooking container: Absorbent Paper
Cooking time: 1½ minutes
Number of servings: 20

1 small can crab meat
2 oz. (50 g) grated cheese
2 teaspoons (10 ml) finely chopped onion
2 teaspoons (10 ml) parsley flakes
1 teaspoon (5 ml) horseradish sauce
1 teaspoon (5 ml) tomato sauce
1 teaspoon (5 ml) Worcestershire sauce
salt to taste
20 small Melba toast squares

Combine all ingredients. Mix well and divide between the toast squares. Place these on a dish lined with a paper doily or towel and heat for [a] 1½ minutes or until the cheese in the mix begins to bubble.

500 watt		650 watt/2 power	
a	2-2½ minutes	a	1-1½ minutes
650 watt			
a	PL.8 for 1½ minutes		

Vol au Vents

These can be cooked from the frozen state in the microwave oven. Method as follows:

1. Place 6 frozen vol au vents onto kitchen paper.
2. Place into the microwave oven and cook for [a] 5¾ minutes or until set when door is opened.
3. Allow to stand on removal from the oven.

3½" vol au vents will not be a golden brown but are ideal for using for quick family meals.

Note: Try placing the vol au vents upside down in the oven as this achieves an even greater rise. When they come out of the oven you can easily turn them the right way up to ensure that the surface is flat. When reheating vol au vents, best results are achieved by heating the filling and pastry separately. Reheat the pastry vol au vents on kitchen paper or a roasting rack and then fill them with the hot filling.

500 watt		650 watt/2 power	
a	6 minutes	a	4½ minutes
650 watt			
a	PL.9 for 4½ minutes		

Savoury Mushrooms

See colour plate page 41
Cooking container: Round plate
Cooking time: 5 minutes
Number of servings: 8

8 large button mushrooms
1 oz. (25 g) breadcrumbs
1 oz. (25 g) stilton cheese
1 oz. (25 g) butter

Remove the stems from the mushrooms and chop finely. Melt the butter in the oven for [a] 1 minute. Sauté the chopped stems for [b] 1 minute. Add the breadcrumbs and crumbled Stilton and mix well. Fill the mushrooms and cook in the oven for [c] 2-3 minutes. Sprinkle with chopped parsley before serving.

500 watt		650 watt/2 power	
a	1 minute	a	30 minutes
b	1½ minutes	b	1 minute
c	3-4 minutes	c	1½-2 minutes
650 watt			
a	PL.9 for 30 seconds		
b	PL.9 for 1 minute		
c	PL.7 for 2-3 minutes		

Bacon Sticks

See colour plate page 41
Cooking container: Roasting rack
Cooking time: 5 minutes
Number of servings:

8 rashers streaky bacon
garlic or celery salt
1 packet bread sticks

Remove rind from bacon and stretch the rashers with the back of a knife; sprinkle with garlic or celery salt. Wrap bacon around bread sticks. Place on absorbent paper or roasting rack and heat for [a] 5-7 minutes until crisp. Serve hot.

500 watt		650 watt/2 power	
a	6-8 minutes	a	4-6 minutes
650 watt			
a	PL.7 for 5-7 minutes		

Frankfurters

Cooking container: Absorbent Paper
Cooking time: 1¾ minutes
Number of servings: 6

1 tin or packet of hot dog sausages
6 finger bread rolls

Drain the frankfurters and place into slit bread rolls.
Place onto absorbent paper and heat for [a] 1½-1¾
minutes. Fried onions can be added to the frankfurters
before heating.

500 watt		650 watt/2 power	
a	2½ minutes	a	1-1½ minutes
650 watt			
a	PL.8 for 1½-1¾ minutes		

Timings to heat one frankfurter in roll is as follows:

500 watt	600 watt
1 minute	40 seconds
650 watt/2 power	650 watt
30 seconds	PL.8 for 35 seconds

Hot Cheese & Onion Rolls

Cooking container: Absorbent Paper
Cooking time: 2½ minutes
Number of servings: 4

4 bread rolls
4 oz. (100 g) sliced cheese
1 large onion thinly sliced
butter

Cut the bread rolls in half and spread lightly with butter.
Divide the onion slices between the bread rolls. Place the
cheese on top of the bread roll and heat on absorbent
paper in the microwave oven for [a] 2½ minutes.

500 watt		650/2 power	
a	3-3½ minutes	a	2 minutes
650 watt			
a	PL.8 for 2½ minutes		

Timings to heat one bread roll with filling are as follows:

500 watt	600 watt
1 minute	45 seconds
650 watt/2 power	650 watt
30 seconds	PL.8 for 45 seconds

Spicy almonds

Spicy Almonds

See colour plate page 41

Cooking container: Shallow dish
Cooking time: 7 minutes
Number of servings:

1 oz. (25 g) butter
1½ teaspoon (7.5 ml) chilli powder
1 teaspoon (5 ml) celery salt
pinch cayenne pepper
½ teaspoon (2.5 ml) salt
8 oz. (225 g) whole blanched almonds

Melt butter in shallow dish then stir in all ingredients.
Heat for [a] 7 minutes stirring twice. Cool on kitchen
paper before serving. Store in an air tight jar.

500 watt		650 watt/2 power	
a	9 minutes	a	6 minutes
650 watt			
a	PL.7 for 7 minutes		

Puppodums

Place 3 puppodums onto the oven tray and heat for [a] 1 minute. Rearrange and heat for a further [b] 45 seconds.

	500 watt		650 watt/2 power
a	1½ minutes	a	45 scconds
b	45 seconds	b	45 seconds
	650 watt		
	a	PL.9 for 45 seconds	
	b	PL.9 for 45 seconds	

Microwave Pastry Case

Cooking container: 8" flan or pie dish
Cooking time: 4½ minutes
Number of servings: 8

4 oz. (100 g) wholemeal flour
2 oz. (50 g) plain flour
1½ oz. (40 g) lard
1½ oz. (40 g) margarine
pinch of salt
2 tablespoons (30 ml) milk

Mix the fat into the flour and salt. Add the milk and mix to form a dough. Roll out on a floured board, brush off excess flour and place into greased flan dish. Damp the edges of the pastry to prevent over-cooking and cover the pastry case completely with kitchen paper. Place a plate or dish slightly less than 8" in diameter onto pastry case and cook for (a) 3½ minutes. Remove top dish and paper, return pastry to oven and cook for a further (b) 1 minute.

	500 watt		650 watt/2 power
a	4½ minutes	a	3½ minutes
b	1 minute	b	30 seconds
	650 watt		
	a	PL.9 for 3½ minutes	
	b	PL.9 for 30 seconds	

Bacon & Egg Flan

Cooking container: 8" flan or pie dish
Cooking time: 17¼ minutes
Number of servings: 6-8

1 x 8" cooked pastry case
1 onion finely chopped
4 oz. (100 g) bacon cut into small pieces
4 oz. (100 g) mushrooms
3 large eggs
8 fl. oz. (240 ml) milk
1 tablespoon (15 ml) oil
salt and pepper
paprika
1 tomato

Put oil in bowl and heat for [a] 45 seconds. Add the chopped onion and cook for a further [b] 3½ minutes. Remove from oven and leave to stand for 5 minutes. Place bacon between two pieces of kitchen paper or on a rack covered with kitchen paper and cook for [c] 4 minutes. Take out and leave to one side. Warm the milk for [d] 2 minutes in the oven. Whisk eggs, salt and pepper and add warm milk. Place mushrooms in the base of the flan then add the onions and bacon. Pour the egg mixture over and decorate with sliced tomato. Sprinkle with paprika and cook for [e] 7-8 minutes. Allow to stand for 10 minutes before serving.

	500 watt		650 watt/2 power
a	1 minutes	a	30 seconds
b	4 minutes	b	3 minutes
c	4½-5 minutes	c	3½ minutes
d	2½ minutes	d	2 minutes
e	8-10 minutes (turn once)	e	6-7 minutes
	650 watt		
	a	PL.9 for 30 seconds	
	b	PL.8 for 3 minutes	
	c	PL.9 for 3½ minutes	
	d	PL.9 for 2 minutes	
	e	PL.9 for 3 minutes PL.7 for 4 minutes	

Drinks

Drinks

Favourite hot drinks are quick with the microwave oven and all can be heated in a cup, mug or glass, saving on washing up. Even tea or cold coffee can be reheated in the microwave to give it a hot fresh flavour.

As a general rule:

1 Heat drinks in glass, ceramic, pottery, plastic mugs or cups, but make sure there is no metal trim.
2 When heating individual cups there is no need to cover.
3 When heating large quantities of drinks in the oven, it is often easier to heat in one container and then pour into mugs.
4 In a variable power oven heat on high power, level 9 unless the drink contains milk, then use power level 7 (roast).

Microwave method

Heating drinks is a matter of bringing the liquid temperature up to the required serving temperature. Serving temperature is a matter of personal taste, so you may find timings need to be increased or decreased depending on how hot you want the drinks.

To heat a drink in the microwave oven

1 Fill the cup or mug to the required level, place the cup into the oven and heat for the suggested time.
2 If adding a granule substance after heating, such as granular coffee or sugar to the liquid, allow the liquid to stand for just a few moments, add the coffee or sugar, stir and serve.

Heating Liquids in the Microwave Oven to boiling Point

	Quantity	500 watt mins	600 watt mins	650 watt/PL.9 mins
Water	1 cup	2½	1¾-2	1½-1¾
	2 cups	4½-4¾	3-3½	3
	1 mug	3½	2¾	2¾-3
	2 mugs	5-6	5	4½
	1 pint	7¾-8	6-7	6-6¼
	1½ pints	14	12	9-10
	2 pints	17	14	13¾-14
Milk	1 cup	2	2	1¾-2
	2 cups	3¼	3¼	2¾-3
	1 mug	3-3¼	2½-2¾	2½
	2 mugs	5½-6	4½	3½
	1 pint	7	6	4-4½
	1½ pints	10-11	8-9	6-6½
	2 pints	13-14	10-11	8-9

N.B. Cup size = 5 fl. oz. (150 ml)
   Mug size = 8 fl. oz. (230 ml)

The temperature probe can be used bery successfully for heating up a cup or mug of water or milk. Suggested temperature is 70°C-80°C depending on individual taste.

Japanese Punch

Cooking container: 3 pint container
Cooking time: 3½ minutes
Number of servings: 6-8 glasses

½ pint (275 ml) tea
4 cloves
1 cinnamon stick
½ teaspoon (2.5 ml) ground ginger
2 pints (1.1 litre) lemonade
small sprig mint

Heat the tea, cloves, cinnamon stick, ginger and mint for [a] 3½ minutes. Leave to cool. Strain the tea and stir in lemonade. Serve chilled.

	500 watt		650 watt/2 power
a	4-4½ minutes	a	3 minutes
	650 watt		
	a	PL.9 for 3 minutes	

Mulled Ale

Cooking container: 3 pint container
Cooking time: 9 minutes
Number of servings: 2-3

1 pint (550 ml) pale ale
1 tablespoon (15 ml) sugar
1 cinnamon stick
pinch ground ginger
peeled rind and juice one orange
3 tablespoons (15 ml) rum

Combine all ingredients into container. Heat in the oven to dissolve sugar for about [a] 5 minutes. Stir well and leave to stand for 15 minutes. Return to the oven for [b] 4 minutes before serving. The ale can be strained before serving.

500 watt		650 watt/2 power	
a	6 minutes	a	4 minutes
b	5 minutes	b	3½ minutes
650 watt			
a	PL.7 for 5 minutes		
b	PL.9 for 3½ minutes		

Temp Probe: **b** 75°C, PL.9

Hot Banana Honey

Cooking container: 2 pint container
Cooking time: 4 minutes
Number of servings: 2

2 large bananas
1 pint (550 ml) milk
Honey to taste
Vanilla essence

Mash bananas well; heat milk for [a] 4 minutes. Mix with bananas, add honey and vanilla essence to taste.

500 watt		650 watt/2 power	
a	5-5½ minutes	a	3½-4 minutes
650 watt			
a	PL.8 for 4 minutes		

Temp Probe: **a** 80°C, PL.8

Hot Beef & Tomato Savoury

Cooking container: 1 pint container
Cooking time: 4 minutes
Number of servings: 2-3 cups

¼ pint (150 ml) tomato juice
½ pint (275 ml) beef stock
salt and pepper

Combine stock and juice, season to taste and heat for [a] 4 minutes. Stir and serve.

500 watt		650 watt/2 power	
a	6 minutes	a	3¼ minutes
650 watt			
a	PL.9 for 3¾ minutes		

Temp Probe: **a** 75°C, PL.9

Instant Coffee

Cooking container: Mug
Cooking time: 1¾ minutes
Number of servings: 1

7 fl. oz. (210 ml) water
instant coffee

Fill a mug with water, approximately 7 fl. oz. Heat in the oven for [a] 1¾ minutes. Add the instant coffee granules and milk and sweeten as required.

500 watt		650 watt/2 power	
a	3-3½ minutes	a	1½ minutes
650 watt			
a	PL.9 for 1½ minutes		

Temp Probe: **a** 80°C, PL.9

Mulled Wine

See colour plate page 49

Cooking container: 3 pint casserole
Cooking time: 6 minutes
Number of servings: 6-8 cups

2 pints (1.1 litre) red wine
one cinnamon stick
5 tablespoons (75 ml) sugar
good pinch of nutmeg

Mix all ingredients together and heat in the microwave oven for approximately [a] 5-6 minutes. Stir once during this cycle. Serve hot with orange slices.

500 watt		650 watt/2 power	
a	7-8 minutes	a	4-5 minutes
650 watt			
a	PL.9 for 4-5 minutes		

Temp Probe: **a** 75°C, PL.9

Fizzy Orange

Cooking container: 3 pint container
Cooking time: 3½ minutes
Number of servings: 3 glasses

2 oz. (50 g) sugar
½ pint (275 ml) fresh orange juice (chilled)
4 tablespoons (60 ml) water
1 tablespoon (15 ml) lemon juice
½ pint (275 ml) soda or tonic water (chilled)

Heat the sugar and water for [a] 3½ minutes, stir to dissolve. Cool and add all other ingredients.

500 watt		650 watt/2 power	
a	4-4½ minutes	a	3 minutes
650 watt			
a	PL.7 for 4 minutes		

Hot Chocolate

Cooking container: Mug
Cooking time: 2½ minutes
Number of servings: 1

1 mug of milk
3 teaspoons (15 ml) drinking chocolate
1 marshmallow

Heat milk in mug for [a] 2 minutes. Stir in chocolate. Top with marshmallow and heat for [b] 30 seconds.

500 watt		650 watt/2 power	
a	3 minutes	a	2 minutes
b	45 seconds	b	30 seconds
650 watt			
a	PL.7 for 2½ minutes		
b	PL.7 for 1 minute		

Temp Probe: **a** 65°C, PL.7
　　　　　　 b 75°C, PL.7

Irish Coffee

Cooking container: Mug
Cooking time: 2½ minutes
Number of servings: 1

7 fl. oz. (210 ml) strong black coffee
brown sugar
1 measure whisky
cream

Heat coffee in mug for [a] 2½ minutes. Stir in sugar and whisky. Using a cold metal spoon, top with cream.

500 watt		650 watt/2 power	
a	3 minutes	a	2½ minutes
650 watt			
a	PL.9 for 2½ minutes		

Temp Probe: a 80°C, PL.9

Tea

Cooking container: Cup
Cooking time: 1¾-2 minutes
Number of servings: 1

1 tea bag
5fl. oz. (150 ml) water

Place one cup containing approximately 5 fl. oz. water into the microwave oven. Heat for [a] 1¾-2 minutes or until vigorously boiling. Drop in tea bag and allow the tea to stand for a couple of minutes before removing tea bag.

500 watt		650 watt/2 power	
a	2½ minutes	a	1½-2 minutes
650 watt			
a	PL.9 for 1½-2 minutes		

Mulled wine P.49

Sauces

Whether you are making a packet sauce or one from fresh ingredients, all you need is a wire whisk and a large bowl for lump free results.

As a general rule:

1 Use a large bowl.
2 Use a wire whisk for stirring.
3 Cook uncovered.
4 Stir at least once or twice during cooking time.

Microwave method:

1 Sauces using cornflour
   Combine all ingredients, cook in oven until boiling, whisk and serve..

2 Sauces using flour
   a Melt fat
   b Add flour
   c Add liquid — whisk and heat to boiling
   d Whisk and serve

Variable power ovens

Cook milk, cream and egg based sauces on power level 7.

Instant Sauce Mixes

1 Empty powder into a 1 pint bowl.
2 Stir with a little of the milk as directed on packet.
3 Heat the rest of the milk in the microwave oven for [a] 2 minutes.
4 Pour onto the powder, stirring well.
5 Return the sauce to the oven for another [b] 2 minutes, stirring well halfway through the cooking cycle.
6 Serve or use as required. Instructions are for a ½ pint packet mix.

	500 watt		650 watt/2 power
a	3 minutes	a	2 minutes
b	3 minutes	b	3 minutes

	650 watt	
	a	PL.9 for 2 minutes
	b	PL.9 for 3 minutes

Gravy

See colour plate page 59

Cooking container: 1 pint bowl
Cooking time: 5 minute
Number of servings: 4-5

1 oz. (25 g) meat dripping
½ pint (275 ml) meat or vegetable stock
1 level tablespoon (15 ml) flour
2 teaspoons (10 ml) gravy mix
seasoning

Heat the stock for [a] 2 minutes. Melt the dripping in the oven for [b] 30 seconds, add to it the flour and gravy mix, stir well and heat for [c] 30 seconds. Pour in the liquid stock, mix to a smooth paste and heat in the oven for [d] 2 minutes. Stir briskly halfway through this cycle. Season as required before serving.

	500 watt		650 watt/2 power
a	3 minutes	a	2 minutes
b	1 minute	b	30 seconds
c	1 minute	c	15 seconds
d	5 minutes	d	1¾-2 minutes

	650 watt	
	a	PL.9 for 2 minutes
	b	PL.7 for 30 seconds
	c	PL.7 for 30 seconds
	d	PL.8 for 2 minutes

Apple Sauce

See colour plate page 59

Cooking container: 2 pint bowl
Cooking time: 5 minutes
Number of servings: 4-6
8 oz. (225 g) cooking apples
½ oz. (15 g) butter
sugar to taste

Peel, core and slice the apples. Place in a covered container in the oven with 1 tablespoon of water. Cook in the microwave oven for [a] 5 minutes (this timing will vary slightly with the type of apple used, but they should be soft when removed from the oven). Remove from oven and stir until smooth, add the butter and sugar and mix well. Stand covered for 5 minutes before using.

	500 watt		650 watt/2 power
a	6 minutes	a	4½ minutes

	650 watt	
	a	PL.9 for 4½ minutes

A selection of Sauces P.59

White Sauce (Coating Consistency)

See colour plate page 59

Cooking container: 2 pint bowl
Cooking time: 6 minutes
Number of servings: 4

1 oz. (25 g) flour
1 oz (25 g) butter
½ pint (275 ml) milk
seasoning

Heat the milk in the oven for [a] 2 minutes. Melt the butter in a separate container for [b] 30 seconds. Stir the flour into the butter and cook for [c] 1 minute. Remove from oven and gradually pour the milk into the flour mix, stirring well. Return to oven for [d] 45 seconds, stir or whisk and cook for a further [e] 45 seconds. Season to taste. Additional ingredients i.e. cheese can be added to the sauce at this stage. Stir well. Cook for a further [f] 1½ minutes before serving.

For a thinner sauce less flour and fat should be used; for a thicker sauce increase the amounts. Timings will be altered correspondingly.

	500 watt		650 watt/2 power
a	3 minutes	a	1¾ minutes
b	1 minute	b	30 seconds
c	2 minutes	c	30 seconds
d	2 minutes	d	30 seconds
e	1 minute	e	45 seconds
f	2 minutes	f	1 minute

	650 watt
a	PL.9 for 1¾ minutes
b	PL.9 for 30 seconds
c	PL.7 for 1 minute
d	PL.9 for 30 seconds
e	PL.9 for 45 seconds
f	PL.9 for 1 minute

Quickie Tomato Sauce

See colour plate page 59

Cooking container: 2 pint basin
Cooking time: 12½ minutes
Number of servings: 6

14 oz. (397 g) tin chopped tomatoes
½ oz. (15 g) margarine
small finely chopped onion
¼ pint (150 ml) chicken stock
salt
pepper
½ teaspoon (2.5 g) sugar
good pinch marjoram
1 tablespoon (15 ml) tomato puree
1 teaspoon (5 g) cornflour

Place the onion and fat into a 2 pint basin and cook for [a] 2½ minutes. Add all other ingredients except tomato puree and cornflour. Stir well and cook for [b] 5 minutes. Add to sauce one tablespoon tomato puree and one teaspoon of cornflour mixed with a little water. Return to the oven and cook for a further [c] 5 minutes. Stir once or twice during this cycle. If desired the sauce can be placed into blender or food processor to be made smooth for serving.

	500 watt		650 watt/2 power
a	3 minutes	a	2½ minutes
b	6 minutes	b	5 minutes
c	5-6 minutes	c	5 minutes

	650 watt
a	PL.7 for 4 minutes
b	PL.9 for 4 minutes
c	PL.9 for 4 minutes

Sweet & Sour Sauce

See colour plate page 59

Cooking container: Sauce Boat
Cooking time: 6 minutes
Number of servings: 4-5

2 level tablespoons (30 ml) cornflour
3 tablespoons (45 ml) soft brown sugar
½ teaspoon (2.5 ml) ginger
1 teaspoon (5 ml) paprika
3 tablespoons (45 ml) vinegar
8 oz. (225 g) can pineapple pieces
2 teaspoons (10 ml) soy sauce
2 teaspoons (10 ml) redcurrant jelly
6 tablespoons (90 ml) water

Drain pineapple. Combine in sauce boat the juice of the pineapple (add pieces later) and all other ingredients. Heat in oven for [a] 4 minutes, stirring every minute. Add pineapple pieces and heat for [b] 2 minutes. Stir and use as required.

	500 watt		650 watt/2 power
a	6 minutes	a	3½ minutes
b	3 minutes	b	2 minutes

	650 watt	
a	PL.9 for 3½ minutes	
b	PL.9 for 2 minutes	

Bread Sauce

Cooking container: 3 pint bowl
Cooking time: 9½ minutes
Number of servings: 6-8

2 cloves
1 medium onion, peeled
a few peppercorns
salt
¾ pint (425 ml) milk
3 oz. (75 g) white breadcrumbs
½ oz. (15 g) butter

Heat the milk with the peppercorns and onion stuck with cloves for [a] 3½ minutes. Stand to one side for 20 minutes. Remove the peppercorns, add the breadcrumbs and butter, and heat in the oven for [b] 6 minutes. Stir once during this cycle. Remove the onion, add salt to taste, stir and allow to stand before serving.

	500 watt		650 watt/2 power
a	4 minutes	a	3 minutes
b	12 minutes	b	5 minutes

	650 watt	
a	PL.9 for 3 minutes	
b	PL.8 for 5½ minutes	

Curry Sauce

Cooking container: 2 pint bowl
Cooking time: 20 minutes
Number of servings: 4-5

1 oz. (25 g) fat
1 large onion, finely chopped
1 tablespoon (15 ml) curry powder
1 level tablespoon (15 ml) flour
½ pint (275 ml) stock
2 tablespoons (30 ml) chutney
½ teaspoon (2.5 ml) garlic salt
pinch cayenne pepper

Place the onion with the fat in the oven for [a] 6 minutes. Add the flour and curry powder to the onion, mix well and cook for [b] 2½ minutes. Gradually pour in the stock, mix until smooth and cook in the oven for [c] 3 minutes. Add all other ingredients, season to taste and cook covered in the oven for [d] 8½ minutes. Stir once or twice during the cycle. Stir on removal from oven, check seasoning and allow to stand for 10 minutes before serving. Heat as required.

	500 watt		650 watt/2 power
a	7½ minutes	a	5½ minutes
b	3 minutes	b	2 minutes
c	3½-4 minutes	c	2½ minutes
d	10 minutes	d	7 minutes

	650 watt	
a	PL.7 for 6 minutes	
b	PL.7 for 2½ minutes	
c	PL.9 for 2½ minutes	
d	PL.9 for 7 minutes	

Hollandaise Sauce

Cooking container: 2 pint bowl
Cooking time: 2½-3½ minutes
Number of servings: 3-4

2 tablespoons (30 ml) wine vinegar
1 tablespoon (15 ml) water
2 egg yolks
4 oz. (100 g) butter, cubed
seasoning

Heat the water and vinegar together in the oven for [a] 2 minutes. Stir the butter into the vinegar and beat well. Add the egg yolks and whisk until the ingredients are combined together. Heat in the oven for [b] 15-30 seconds and whisk in the seasoning; if not quite thick enough, return to the oven for a further minute. Stand covered for 2 minutes before serving. Care must be taken when reheating this sauce as the egg will curdle if it is boiled.

	500 watt		650 watt/2 power
a	3 minutes	a	2 minutes
b	1 minute	b	20-30 seconds
650 watt			
a	PL.9 for 2 minutes		
b	PL.5 for 1½-2½ minutes		

Egg Custard Sauce

Cooking container: 2 pint bowl
Cooking time: 4½ minute
Number of servings: 3-4

1 tablespoon (15 ml) sugar
2 large eggs
½ pint (275 ml) milk
1 teaspoon (5 ml) grated lemon rind

Heat the milk and lemon rind in the oven for [a] 2 minutes. Whisk the eggs and sugar lightly together. Pour the milk onto the eggs, stir, strain the custard and place in the oven for [b] 2½ minutes until it begins to thicken. Whisk well twice during this cycle. Leave to stand for a few minutes before serving.

	500 watt		650 watt/2 power
a	2½ minutes	a	2 minutes
b	3 minutes	b	2 minutes
650 watt			
a	PL.7 for 2½ minutes		
b	PL.5 for 3½-4 minutes		

Chocolate Sauce for Ice-cream

Cooking container: 1 pint bowl
Cooking time: 1 minute
Number of servings: 4

2 oz. (50 g) plain dark chocolate
1 tablespoon (15 ml) milk
½ oz. (15 g) butter

Break the chocolate into a bowl with the butter. Heat in the oven for [a] 1 minute. Add the milk, stir until smooth and serve. This sauce can be heated gently as required.

	500 watt		650 watt/2 power
a	3 minutes	a	1 minute
650 watt			
a	PL.8 for 1 minute		

Custard

Cooking container: 3 pint bowl
Cooking time: 6½ minutes
Number of servings: 4-5

2 tablespoons (30 ml) custard powder
1 tablespoon (15 ml) sugar
1 pint (550 ml) milk

Mix sugar, powder and a little of the milk to a smooth paste. Heat the remainder of the milk in the oven for [a] 5 minutes. Pour on to the custard powder, stirring well. Return to the oven for [b] 1½-2 minutes. Stir before serving.

	500 watt		650 watt/2 power
a	4 minutes	a	4-5 minutes
b	2 minutes	b	1-1½ minutes
650 watt			
a	PL.9 for 4-5 minutes		
b	PL.9 for 1-1½ minutes		

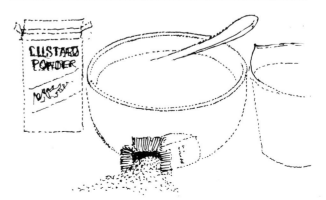

Meats

Meats

Meat cooked in the microwave oven retains all its natural juices and flavour and the oven is easy to clean after cooking. Large joints of meat will colour naturally in the microwave oven but smaller items such as chops and steaks will need to be browned after cooking or cooked in a browning dish.

Many types of meat are appropriate for microwave cooking, but just as with conventional cooking less tender cuts of meat will require a longer cooking time at a slower speed, the same applies in a microwave oven. Although your oven may have only two power levels, you will notice that we have suggested cooking different cuts of meat on defrost power. Where you have a variable power oven, then we have noted the power levels that different types of meat should be cooked on.

As a general rule:

1 Best cooking results are achieved when meat is at room temperature rather than refrigerated.
2 After defrosting joints of meat in the oven it is advisable to allow at least 30 minutes resting time before cooking.
3 Always use a roasting rack suitable for the microwave oven.
4 A meat thermometer. either one contained in the oven in the form of a probe or one designed for use in a microwave oven is a must for roasting meats to the perfect degree.
5 Cover meats when simmering.
6 Always roast meat fat side down and turn over once halfway through the cooking time.

Microwave method for roasting:

Use the procedure below in conjunction with the meat roasting charts for roasting all types of meat.
1 Place meat onto roasting rack fat side down. If the joint is an awkward shape such as a leg of lamb, then shield the end of the lamb with a piece of foil.
2 Add the required seasoning to the meat.
3 Cover with a slit roasting bag.
4 Place the meat into the oven and cook as directed on roasting chart. With large joints of meat it is advisable to turn them over halfway through the cooking time.
Note: When using a microwave thermometer, this should be placed into the centre of the joint so that the temperature there can be recorded. Make sure that the tip of the thermometer is not touching any bone in the meat.

5 Take the joint out of the oven when it has reached the correct temperature or time. Cover with foil and allow to stand for 20 minutes before carving. This allows the meat to finish cooking and make sure that it is easier to carve. The meat will not lose any temperature in this time, in fact, it will rise.

Microwave method for small items of meat:
Small items of meat such as hamburgers, steaks, chops which are going to be covered with sauce or placed under the grill after cooking can be cooked in the oven in the following method.

Meat
1 Place items of meat onto a roasting rack.
2 Season or add colouring.
3 Cover with a slit roasting bag.
4 Cook in the microwave oven for the time and at the power level as directed on the chart.
5 Remember that the food must be left to stand when it comes out of the microwave oven.

Joint of beef on a roasting rack

Microwave method for minced meat:
Minced meat is tender and can either be cooked in meatballs, hamburgers or as a minced beef casserole. To brown the meat for the casserole, the following procedure can be used. Separate the meat into a suitable dish. Cook on full power or power level 7 for 6 minutes or until it loses its pink colour. Drain and then add vegetables or mix it into hamburgers.

Microwave method for casseroles:
Meat for casseroles can either be browned on top of your conventional cooker before placing into the microwave oven or can be done by the following method. Place meat into glass dish or onto roasting rack. Cook on power level 7 or on full power until the meat loses its pink colour. The fat can either be drained from the meat or add other casserole ingredients and carry on cooking. There are several casserole recipes in this section so follow these for the required timing.

Meat
Joints normally cooked in stock or water such as pot roast or a gammon joint — for these follow normal cooking procedure but inside the oven. Again use a temperature probe as this helps to ensure that the meat is taken out of the oven at the right time. If doing a pot roast which is normally browned before cooking, it is suggested that it is done in a frying pan. Bring the water up to the boil in the oven with the meat in it and then turn down to defrost or simmer.

Microwave Method for Bacon/Gammon:-
Bacon can be cooked in the microwave oven in two different ways. Either place the slices onto a roasting rack or paper towel as shown in the picture. Cover with a paper towel and cook in the microwave oven to the required degree of crispness. Times again given in the meat cooking chart. Gammon steaks can be done by the same method. If you want to add a sauce to the steak, then halfway through cooking time drain off the extra liquid and place onto serving dish. Add sauce and continue cooking in the microwave oven.

Cooked joint of Beef

Joints of Meat
Cooking and standing time mins per lb (450 g)
When using variable power ovens, cook for 2 minutes per lb on PL.9 then follow the chart.

Item	500 watt	600 watt	650 watt/ 2 power	650 watt	Temp.	Standing time
Beef	8	6	6	PL.4 for 7-8	130°F 55°C (rare)	5
	9	7	7	PL.4 for 9-10	145°F 65°C (medium)	
	11	8½	8	PL.4 for 12-13	160°F 70°C (well done)	
Pork	12	9	9	PL.7 for 9	175°F 80°C	5
Lamb	10	8	8	PL.7 for 7-8	160°F 70°C	5
Breast of Lamb stuffed and rolled	12	9	8½	PL.7 for 11	145°F 65°C	5
Gammon/bacon (pour ⅓ pt water into roasting rack)	12	10	9	PL.7 for 9	145°F 65°C	5

Small Cuts of Meat

Approx. cooking and standing time mins per lb (450 g)

Item	500 watt	600 watt	650 watt/ 2 power	650 watt	Standing time
Bacon	12	10	8	PL.9 for 8	3
Gammon Steak	18	16	14	PL.9 for 15	3
Hamburgers	12-14	8-10	7-8	PL.7 for 10-12	5
Sausages	8-9	6-7	6	PL.7 for 7	5
Liver	7-8	5-6	5	PL.7 for 7	5
Kidneys	8-10	6-8	6	PL.7 for 8	5
Mincemeat	22	18	15-17	PL.7 for 20	10
Lamb chops	10-12	8-10	8-9	PL.7 for 9-11	5
Pork chops	12-14	8-12	10	PL.7 for 8-12	5

Timing will depend on thickness and the degree of cooking required. Meat can be pre-coloured in a frying pan, under a grill, using a browning griddle or sprinkled with seasoning.

Meat Cookery with the Temperature Probe

The temperature probe ensures the meat is cooked to the required degree without you working out "how many minutes per lbs"

Prepare the meat for roasting as on page 64:

1. Insert the temperature probe into the joint horizontally so that the tip is in the centre of the joint. The probe should run parallel to any bones.

2. Cover the joint with a slit roasting bag.

3. Place meat into oven and connect probe.

4. Programme oven as suggested on chart.

5. Meat should be turned over when the temperature reaches 50°C.

6. Leave to stand before carving.

Temperature Probe Cooking Chart for Joints of Meat

Note: All joints are cooked on 2 separate power levels to 2 separate temperatures

Food Item	Temperature Setting	Power Level	Standing Time
Beef			
Rare to medium	50°C	7	5 mins per lb
	60°C	4	
Medium to well done	50°C	7	5 mins per lb
	75°C	4	
Lamb			
Pink	50°C	7	5 mins per lb
	70°C	4	
Well done	50°C	7	5 mins per lb
	75°C	4	
Pork			
Well done	50°C	7	5 mins per lb
	80°C	4	
Veal	50°C	7	5 mins per lb
	75°C	4	
Gammon/Bacon	50°C	7	5 mins per lb
	65°C	4	

Casseroles or Slow Cooking with the Temperature Probe

Using the temperature probe in conjunction with the Heat and Hold control, it is possible to cook for a long period without boiling.

The same effect on food as slow cooking in a conventional oven or slow cooker can be achieved. The cooking times are similar too. Several of the recipes in this section and the Poultry section suggest final cooking on Heat and Hold. It will be noticed that the suggested Heat and Hold time is often a lot longer than on separate power levels, this is because the cooking temperature is being controlled. The Heat and Hold time is a guideline only and can be increased to suit your own taste.

Microwave method for Heat and Hold Cooking

Prepare casserole as stated in recipe, using a deep casserole dish rather than a shallow one. Insert probe into oven socket and place the tip of the probe into the centre or halfway down into the liquid. Note: It is important to have the probe tip only recording the temperature of the liquid and not be inserted into the meat or vegetables. Cover dish with lid or cling film. Programme oven as suggested in recipe. Remember, all times suggested on Heat and Hold are minimum amounts.

Crown of Lamb

Cooking container: Roasting Rack
Cooking time: Approx. 40 minutes
Number of servings: 6-8

1 crown of lamb
1 oz. (25 g) butter
1 chopped onion
6 oz. (150 g) chopped celery
4 oz. (100 g) apricots, cooked and chopped
8 oz. (225 g) cooked long grain rice
1 tablespoon (15 ml) chopped parsley
stock
salt and pepper

Place the butter, onion and celery into a covered container, cook for [a] 8 minutes. Stir in apricots, parsley, rice, salt and pepper. Moisten with stock. Place the crown onto roasting rack, fill with stuffing. Cover the top with buttered paper. Cook for [b] 8 minutes per lb including stuffing weight. Stand covered for 15 minutes before serving.

500 watt Not Suitable		650 watt/2 power	
		a	6½ minutes per lb
		b	8-8½ minutess per lb
650 watt			
a	PL.9 for 6½ minutes		
b	PL.9 for 2 minutes per lb		
	PL.7 for 7 minutes per lb		

Temp probe: **b** 70°C, PL.7 — Pink
75°C, PL.7 — Well done

Cottage Pie

Cooking container: Round baker
Cooking time: 12 minutes
Number of servings: 4

12 oz. (350 g) cooked meat finely minced
1 onion, chopped
¼ pint (150 ml) stock
½ oz. (15 g) margarine
seasoning
1 lb (450 g) mashed potatoes

Melt the margarine in the oven for [a] 1 minute, sauté the onion for [b] 2 minutes. Mix with the meat and stock. Season to taste. Place into dish and cover with the potato. Cook in the oven for [c] 9 minutes. Place under the grill to brown before serving.

500 watt		650 watt/2 power	
a	1½ minutes	a	30 seconds
b	3 minutes	b	2 minutes
c	10 minutes	c	7 minutes
650 watt			
a	PL.7 for 1 minute		
b	PL.7 for 2 minutes		
c	PL.8 for 8 minutes		

Savoury Mince

Cooking container: 3 pint casserole
Cooking time: 40 minutes
Number of servings: 4

1 lb (450 g) minced beef
½ oz. (15 g) butter
1 chopped onion
2 chopped carrots
4 oz. (100 g) chopped mushrooms
¾ pint (425 ml) beef stock
2 teaspoons (10 ml) chopped parsley
½ teaspoon (2.5 ml) celery salt
1 tablespoon (15 ml) tomato puree
1½ tablespoons (25 ml) porridge oats
salt and pepper

Sauté the carrots and onions with the butter for [a] 5 minutes. Mix in the mushrooms and the minced beef and cook for [b] 5 minutes. Stir well after 3 minutes. Add all other ingredients except for the salt and pepper, cover and cook for [c] 30 minutes on defrost power. Remove from the oven and check the seasoning.

	500 watt		650 watt/2 power
a	5 minutes	a	5 minutes
b	5 minutes	b	5 minutes
c	18 minutes	c	35 minutes on defrost
	650 watt		
	a	PL.7 for 5 minutes	
	b	PL.9 for 5 minutes	
	c	PL.3 for 30 minutes	

Temp Probe: H & H 90°C for minimum of 2 hours.

Curry

Cooking container: 2½ pint casserole
Cooking time: 34 minutes
Number of servings: 3-4

12 oz. (350 g) cooked meat
2 tablespoons (30 ml) coconut
1 tablespoon (15 ml) water
1 onion, chopped
1 apple, peeled, cored and sliced
1 oz. (25 g) margarine
1 tablespoon (15 ml) curry powder — depending on taste
2 oz. (50 g) flour
¾ pint (425 ml) stock
2 oz. (50 g) sultanas
1 tablespoon (15 ml) tomato puree
½ teaspoon (2.5 ml) sugar
½ teaspoon (2.5 ml) salt
1 tablespoon (15 ml) lemon juice

Heat coconut for [a] 2 minutes in water. Sauté the onion and the apple in the margarine for [b] 5 minutes. Add the flour and curry, mix well, gradually add the stock and heat for [c] 5 minutes, stirring twice. Add all other ingredients, stir, cover and heat for [d] 22 minutes on defrost. Stir once during this cycle. Stand for 5 minutes before serving.

Suitable for freezing.

	500 watt		650 watt/2 power
a	2 minutes	a	1¾ minutes
b	7 minutes	b	5 minutes
c	5 minutes	c	4 minutes
d	22 minutes	d	25 minutes
	650 watt		
	a	PL.7 for 2 minutes	
	b	PL.7 for 7 minutes	
	c	PL.9 for 4 minutes	
	b	PL.5 for 15 minutes	

Temp Probe: **d** H & H 90°C for 20 minutes

Steak au Poivre

Cooking container: Browning dish
Cooking time: 5½ minutes for medium to well done
2 minutes for rare to medium
Number of servings: 2

2 thick sirloin steaks
1 tablespoon (15 ml) crushed black peppercorns
¾ oz. (20 g) butter
1 tablespoon (15 ml) brandy
2 tablespoons (30 ml) double cream
salt

Heat the browning dish for [a] 6 minutes. Dry the steaks with kitchen paper and smear with butter. Press the peppercorns well into the steaks. When the dish is heated, press the steaks well into the dish and cook for [b] 2 minutes, turn the steaks over and cook for [c] 2 minutes. Remove the steaks from the dish and pour in brandy. Heat for [d] 1 minute. Gradually stir in the cream and the salt. Heat for a further [e] 30 seconds, pour over the steaks and serve. This will give you a medium to well done steak. For a medium to rare steak the timing will be 1 minute on one side and 1 minute on the other side.

	500 watt		650 watt/2 power
a	7 minutes	a	6 minutes
b	2½ minutes	b	2 minutes
c	2 minutes	c	1-2 minutes
d	1 minute	d	30 seconds
e	1 minute	e	45 seconds

650 watt	
a	PL.8 for 6 minutes
b	PL.9 for 2 minutes
c	PL.9 for 1-2 minutes
d	PL.9 for 30 seconds
e	PL.9 for 45 seconds

Beef Casserole

Cooking container: Large casserole
Cooking time: 2 hours 26 minutes
Number of servings: 4

2 oranges
2 lb (900 g) stewing steak, cubed
seasoned flour
1 onion, sliced
1 carrot, sliced
1 oz. (25 g) margarine
1 pint (550 ml) stock
bouquet garni
12 stuffed olives

Squeeze oranges and grate rind. Mix together and marinate the meat in this for 2 hours. Drain and keep the juice. Dip the meat in the seasoned flour. Sauté the onion and carrots with the margarine for [a] 4 minutes in a large casserole. Add meat and cook for [b] 5 minutes. Stir and cook for a further [c] 5 minutes. Add juices, stock and bouquet garni, cover and cook for [d] 12 minutes. Turn down to defrost for [e] 1 hour. Stir and cook for a further [f] 1 hour. Add stuffed olives 20 minutes before end of cooking time.

500 watt Not suitable		650 watt/2 power
	a	3½ minutes
	b	3½ minutes
	c	5 minutes
	d	10 minutes
	e	1 hour defrost
	f	1 hour defrost

650 watt	
a	PL.7 for 4 minutes
b	PL7 for 5 minutes
c	PL.9 for 5 minutes
d	PL.9 for 10 minutes
e	PL.4 for 60 minutes
f	PL.2 for 60 minutes

Temp Probe: **d, e and f** H & H 90°C for at least 4 hours

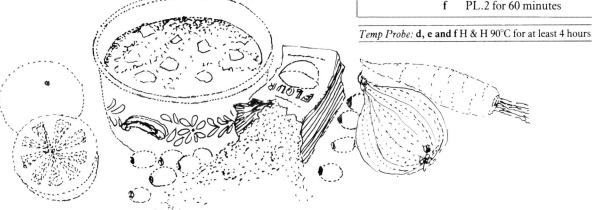

Spicy Meat Loaf

Cooking container: Shallow platter
Cooking time: 17 minutes
Number of servings: 4-5

1 lb (450 g) minced beef
1 medium chopped onion
½ oz. (15 g) margarine
1 egg
½ teaspoon (2.5 ml) salt
1 tablespoon (15 ml) potato powder
1 teaspoon (5 ml) dried parsley
1 teaspoon (5 ml) curry powder
1 teaspoon (5 ml) soy sauce
2 teaspoons (10 ml) Worcestershire sauce
4 oz. (100 g) mushrooms, chopped

Spicy meat loaf

Cook the mushrooms and onion in the margarine for [a] 4 minutes in the oven. Drain off the fat and mix well together with all the other ingredients. Shape into a loaf on a shallow platter. Cover with greaseproof paper and cook in the oven for [b] 6 minutes.

For the Sauce:

Mix together 1 heaped dessertspoon soft dark brown sugar, 1½ teaspoons mustard powder, 1 teaspoon soy sauce, 3 tablespoons chutney and 1 teaspoon curry powder. Spoon the sauce over the meat loaf and cook uncovered in the oven for a further [c] 7 minutes. Leave to stand for 10 minutes before serving.

Suitable for freezing.

	500 watt		650 watt/2 power
a	4 minutes	a	3½ minutes
b	7 minutes	b	6 minutes
c	7-8 minutes	c	6 minutes

	650 watt
a	PL.7 for 4 minutes
b	PL7 for 10 minutes
c	PL.7 for 7 minutes

Chilli con Carne

Cooking container: 3 pint casserole
Cooking time: 46 minutes
Number of servings: 4

15½ oz. (439 g) can red kidney beans, drained
1 lb (450 g) mince
2 onions, chopped
1 pepper, chopped
2 teaspoons (10 ml) oil
2 teaspoons (10 ml) chilli powder
14 oz. (379 g) can tomatoes, chopped
salt
1 tablespoon (15 ml) tomato purée

Heat onion and pepper in oil for [a] 5 minutes in a
covered dish. Add mince, cook for [b] 5 minutes, stir
once during this cycle. Add all other ingredients, cover
and cook for [c] 12 minutes on full power, turn to defrost
and microwave for [d] 24 minutes.

Suitable for freezing.

	500 watt		650 watt/2 power
a	5 minutes	a	4½-5 minutes
b	6 minutes	b	5 minutes
c	24 minutes on defrost	c	10 minutes
d	5 minutes	d	22 minutes on defrost

	650 watt
a	PL.7 for 5 minutes
b	PL.7 for 6 minutes
c	PL.7 for 25 minutes
d	PL.4 for 20 minutes

Temp Probe: **c & d** H & H 90°C for 1½ hours

Savoury Mince Cottage Loaves

Cooking container: Shallow dish
Cooking time: 18½ minutes
Number of servings: 4-6

1 lb (450 g) minced beef
1 large, 2 medium or 4 small fresh crusty cottage loaves
½ 7 oz. (100 g) can baked beans
½ 7 oz. (100 g) can vegetable soup
½ 7 oz. (100 g) can tomatoes
8 oz. (225 g) button mushrooms
2 chopped medium size onions
2 tablespoons (30 ml) Worcestershire sauce
1 tablespoon (15 ml) gravy browning
1 tablespoon (15 ml) mixed herbs
½ teaspoon (2.5 ml) salt
½ teaspoon (2.5 ml) pepper
tomato and parsley for garnish

Place chopped onion in bowl. Cook for [a] 3 minutes.
Hollow out base and tops of cottage loaves. Use the
centres to make breadcrumbs. Reserve half the
breadcrumbs — keep the remaining half in the freezer
for future use. Add all the other ingredients (except the
breadcrumbs) to the onion, stir well and cook for [b] 15
minutes, stirring occasionally. Add the breadcrumbs to
the mixture to thicken. Place hollow loaves on a shallow
dish. Fill with the cooked mixture, replace loaf tops and
return to the oven for [c] 1 minute to heat through. Serve
immediately, garnish with tomato and parsley.

	500 watt		650 watt/2 power
a	4 minutes	a	3 minutes
b	20 minutes	b	12 minutes
c	1 minute	c	30 seconds

	650 watt
a	PL.7 for 3 minutes
b	PL.9 for 12 minutes
c	PL.8 for 45 seconds

Stuffed Marrow

Cooking container: Round dish
Cooking time: 36 minutes
Number of servings: 4

½ oz. (15 g) fat
4 rings marrow 1½" thick, peeled and cored
seasoning
1 large onion, peeled and chopped
1 lb (450 g) mince
2 oz. (50 g) breadcrumbs
4 oz. (100 g) mushrooms, chopped
4 tomatoes, chopped
1 tablespoon (15 ml) tomato purée
grated cheese

Melt fat for [a] 1 minute, brush around marrow rings
and place in a round dish — sprinkle with salt and
pepper. Cook onion for [b] 2 minutes. Add mince and
cook for [c] 2½ minutes, stir and cook for a further [d]
2½ minutes. Add all other ingredients and cook for [e] 7
minutes. Fill marrow rings, cover and cook for [f] 17
minutes. Top with grated cheese and return to oven for
[g] 4 minutes.

	500 watt		650 watt/2 power
a	1½ minutes	a	30 seconds
b	2½ minutes	b	2 minutes
c	3 minutes	c	2 minutes
d	3 minutes	d	2 minutes
e	9 minutes	e	6 minutes
f	20 minutes	f	16 minutes
g	6 minutes	g	4 minutes

	650 watt
a	PL.7 for 1 minute
b	PL.7 for 2 minutes
c	PL.7 for 2½ minutes
d	PL.7 for 2½ minutes
e	PL.5 for 10 minutes
f	PL.9 for 16 minutes
g	PL.9 for 4 minutes

Steak and Kidney Pudding

Cooking container: 1½ pint pudding basin
Cooking time: 48 minutes
Number of servings: 4

8 oz. (225 g) suet pastry
1½ lb (700 g) stewing steak cut into 1" cubes
½ lb (225 g) kidney chopped
1 onion, chopped
pinch herbs
2 fl. oz. (60 ml) gravy made with juices of steak

Marinate stewing steak overnight or sprinkle with meat
tenderiser and leave for 2 hours. Cook meat, kidneys and
onion in casserole dish covered on defrost power for [a]
40 minutes until tender. Stir after 20 minutes and 30
minutes. Grease 1½ pint pudding basin and line with two
thirds of pastry. Add filling and cover with remaining
pastry. Cover with cling wrap and place in oven with cup
of water. Cook for [b] 8 minutes and stand for 1 minute
before serving.

Note: This pudding can be frozen and reheated but the
pastry will not be as good as when freshly cooked.
Additional gravy is required for serving.

	500 watt		650 watt/2 power
a	70 minutes on defrost	a	1 hour on defrost
b	9-10 minutes	b	7 minutes

	650 watt
a	PL.4 for 60 minutes or until tender
b	PL.7 for 8½ minutes

72

Devilled Kidneys

Cooking container: Round baker
Cooking time: 9 minutes
Number of servings: 2-3

8 lambs' kidneys, sliced
1 oz. (25 g) margarine
1 small onion, finely chopped
salt and pepper
1 tablespoon (15 ml) Worcestershire sauce
1 tablespoon (15 ml) dry sherry
1 tablespoon (15 ml) finely chopped parsley

Melt the margarine in the oven for [a] 1 minute, sauté the onion for [b] 2 minutes. Add the seasoning and the kidneys, cook for [c] 2 minutes, stir and cook for a further [d] 2 minutes. Add the sherry, Worcestershire sauce and parsley, cook for [e] 2-3 minutes and stand for 5 minutes. Garnish with croutons before serving.

Suitable for freezing.

	500 watt		650 watt/2 power
a	1½ minutes	a	45 seconds
b	3 minutes	b	2 minutes
c	2 minutes	c	2 minutes
d	3 minutes	d	2 minutes
e	3 minutes	e	2-3 minutes

	650 watt
a	PL.7 for 1 minute
b	PL.7 for 2½ minutes
c	PL.7 for 3 minutes
d	PL.7 for 3 minutes
e	PL.7 for 3-4 minutes

Liver in Spicy Sauce

Cooking container: Browning dish
Cooking time: 9½ minutes
Number of servings: 4

¾ lb (350 g) lambs liver
1 chopped onion
2 Oxo cubes
1 small tin tomato purée
Worcestershire sauce
salt and pepper

Soften the onion in the microwave oven for [a] 1½ minutes. Heat browning dish for [b] 4 minutes. Press liver and onion onto base of skillet — cook for [c] 4 minutes. Turn liver over, add tomato purée plus same amount of water. Crumble in 2 Oxo cubes, add Worcestershire sauce and salt and pepper to taste. Heat covered for [d] 4 minutes.

	500 watt		650 watt/2 power
a	2 minutes	a	1½ minutes
b	6 minutes	b	4 minutes
c	5 minutes	c	2 minutes
d	5 minutes	d	3-4 minutes

	650 watt
a	PL.7 for 2 minutes
b	PL.9 for 4 minutes
c	PL.8 for 2 minutes
d	PL.8 for 4 minutes

Lamb Hotpot

Cooking container: 4 pint casserole
Cooking time: 70 minutes
Number of servings: 4

1½ lb (700 g) best end neck of lamb, chined
¾ lb (350 g) potatoes, thinly sliced
2 onions, chopped
2 large carrots, sliced
salt and pepper
⅓ pint (about 200 ml) dry cider
pinch dried rosemary

Place the lamb into casserole dish, season and sprinkle with the rosemary. Cover with the onions and carrots, pour over the cider and lay the potatoes on top. Cover and cook in the oven for [a] 20 minutes and turn to defrost for [b] 50 minutes. Place under the grill before serving to colour potatoes.

	500 watt		650 watt/2 power
	Not suitable	a	20 minutes
		b	45 minutes defrost

	650 watt
a	PL.5 for 20 minutes
b	PL.2 for 50 minutes

Temp Probe: H & H 90°C for at least 2½ hours

Lamb Casserole

Cooking container: Large casserole dish
Cooking time: 2 hours 35 minutes
Number of servings: 4-6

2 lb (900 g) stewing lamb
2 large onions, chopped
4 carrots, chopped
2 oz. (50 g) pearl barley
2 oz. (50 g) lentils
2½ pints (1.4 litres) water
1 bouquet garni
salt and pepper
3 bay leaves

Heat lentils and barley in 1½ pints of water for [a] 15 minutes. Stand for 1 hour. Place all ingredients into large casserole dish. Cover and place in oven and cook for [b] 20 minutes on full power. Turn to defrost for [c] 2 hours. Leave to stand for 10 minutes before serving.
Suitable for freezing.

500 watt		650 watt/2 power	
Not suitable		a	12 minutes
		b	17 minutes
		c	1¾ hours defrost
650 watt			
	a	PL.9 for 12 minutes	
	b	PL.9 for 17 minutes	
	c	PL.3 for 2¼ hours	

Temp Probe: **b** & **c** H & H 90°C for a minimum of 3 hours

Veal

Cooking container: Browning dish
Cooking time: 4½ minutes
Number of servings: 2

2 veal fillets approximately 4 oz. (100 g)
grated parmesan cheese
seasoned flour
½ oz. (15 g) butter

Heat the browning dish for [a] 5 minutes. Toss the veal in the seasoned flour, add the butter to the browning dish and seal the veal fillets, cook for [b] 1 minute, turn veal fillets over and cook for a further [c] 1 minute. Sprinkle with the cheese, cover with lid and cook for a further [d] 2½ minutes. Leave to stand in dish for a minute or so before serving. ➡

Barbecued Spare Ribs

See colour plate page 75

Cooking container: Roasting dish
Cooking time: 27 minutes
Number of servings: 4

1¼ lb (575 g) spare rib chops
1 finely chopped onion
4 fl. oz. (120 ml) tomato ketchup
1 fl. oz. (30 ml) cider vinegar
1 fl. oz. (30 ml) hot pepper sauce
pinch cayenne pepper
salt
1 level teaspoon (5 ml) mustard
4 tablespoons (60 ml) soft brown sugar
½ oz. (15 g) butter

Colour and seal chops under grill. Sauté onion with butter in dish for [a] 2 minutes. Stir in all other ingredients. Add chops and spoon over sauce. Cook for [b] 5 minutes uncovered. Spoon over sauce and cook for a further [c] 20 minutes on defrost until tender.

	500 watt		650 watt/2 power
a	3 minutes	a	3 minutes
b	6 minutes	b	4 minutes
c	25 minutes	c	20 minutes defrost
650 watt			
a	PL.7 for 2 minutes		
b	PL.9 for 4 minutes		
c	PL.5 for 15-20 minutes		

	500 watt		650 watt/2 power
a	6 minutes	a	5 minutes
b	1½ minutes	b	1 minute
c	2 minutes	c	1 minute
d	3 minutes	d	1½ minutes
650 watt			
a	PL.9 for 5 minutes		
b	PL.7 for 1 minute		
c	PL.7 for 1 minute		
d	PL.7 for 2½ minutes		

Barbecued spare ribs P.75

Duck with Cherry Sauce

Cooking container: Roasting rack
Cooking time for sauce: 53 minutes
Number of servings: 4-5

4 lb (1800 g) cleaned and trussed duck
½ oz. (15 g) butter
8½ oz. (212.5 g) can stoned red cherries
2 tablespoons (30 ml) brandy
2 tablespoons (30 ml) cranberry jelly
rind and juice of one orange
¼ pint (about 150 ml) stock made from giblets
2 teaspoons (10 ml) arrowroot
1 tablespoon (15 ml) water
1 sliced orange (for garnish)

Place the duck, breast down, on a roasting rack and cover loosely with a split roasting bag. Cook for [a] 20 minutes then turn the duck over. Cook for a further [b] 20 minutes (i.e. cook for 10 minutes per lb) and stand, still covered, while sauce is prepared. Melt butter for [c] 1 minute and add cherries. Stir in cranberry jelly, orange juice, rind, brandy and stock. Heat for [d] 4 minutes. Blend arrowroot with water and add to sauce. Cook until sauce thickens (approximately [e] 8 minutes) stirring occasionally. Serve with the duck.

	500 watt		650 watt/2 power
a	24 minutes	a	18 minutes
b	24 minutes	b	20 minutes
c	1½ minutes	c	30 seconds
d	5 minutes	d	3½ minutes
e	10 minutes	e	4 minutes

	650 watt
a	PL.7 for 20 minutes
b	PL.7 for 20 minutes
c	PL.7 for 1 minute
d	PL.9 for 3½ minutes
e	PL9 for 4 minutes

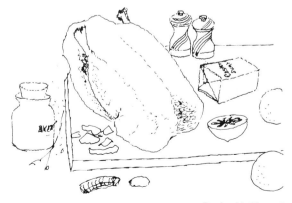

Duck with Cherry Sauce

Duck with Orange Sauce

Cooking container: 2 pint bowl
Cooking time for sauce: 22½ minutes
Number of servings: 4

1 pre-cooked and jointed duck
2 oranges
¼ pint (150 ml) juices from duck giblets
4 fl. oz. (125 ml) red wine vinegar
2 teaspoons (10 ml) caster sugar
1 teaspoon (5 ml) lemon juice
2 teaspoons (10 ml) arrowroot

Cook a 4 lb duck as directed in the recipe for duck and cherries. Wash the oranges and divide them into segments. Cut the peel into thin strips and boil in water for [a] 10 minutes. Drain and place to one side with the orange segments for use later on. Heat vinegar in sugar for [b] 2½ minutes. Stir, then heat vinegar and sugar for a further [c] 5 minutes or until it is reduced. Add the stock and lemon juice. Return to the oven for [d] 4 minutes. Thicken the sauce with the arrowroot and stir until shiny.

	500 watt		650 watt/2 power
a	10 minutes	a	10 minutes
b	4 minutes	b	2 minutes
c	6 minutes	c	4 minutes
d	5 minutes	d	3 minutes

	650 watt
a	PL.9 for 10 minutes
b	PL.9 for 2 minutes
c	PL.9 for 4 minutes
d	PL.9 for 3 minutes

Fish

Creamy Tuna Fish

Cooking container: 2½ pint casserole
Cooking time: 11 minutes   Number of servings: 4

1 oz. (25 g) butter
1 oz. (25 g) flour
¼ red pepper, finely chopped
1 x 7 oz. (198 g) can tuna fish
2 teaspoons (10 ml) capers, rinsed and chopped
12 black olives, stoned and chopped
½ pint (275 ml) milk
salt

Melt the butter in the oven for [a] 1 minute and sauté the peppers for [b] 2 minutes. Stir in the flour and mix well. Return to the oven for [c] 1 minute. Slowly add the milk, stirring well until smooth. Cook in the oven for [d] 3 minutes. Stir well and add the seasoning, flaked tuna fish, olives and capers. Cook covered in the oven for [e] 4 minutes. Stir and serve on hot toast as a snack or starter.

	500 watt		650 watt/2 power
a	1 minute	a	30 seconds
b	3 minutes	b	1½ minutes
c	1 minute	c	1 minute
d	4 minutes	d	2½ minutes
e	6 minutes	e	3 minutes

	650 watt
a	PL.8 for 45 seconds
b	PL.8 for 2 minutes
c	PL.7 for 1 minute
d	PL.7 for 3 minutes
e	PL.8 for 3½ minutes

Special Plaice

Cooking container: Shallow dish
Cooking time: 7¾ minutes
Number of servings: 4

1 lb (450 g) plaice fillet
4 oz. (100 g) frozen prawns
1 oz. (25 g) butter
juice from one lemon
parsley
salt and pepper

Melt the butter in the oven for [a] ¾ minute, add the lemon juice, salt and pepper to the butter. Coat the fish in the butter and place in dish. Sprinkle with prawns and remaining butter. Cover and cook for [b] 7 minutes.

	500 watt		650 watt/2 power
a	1 minute	a	30 seconds
b	8 minutes	b	5½ minutes

	650 watt
a	PL.8 for 45 seconds
b	PL.9 for 6 minutes

Plaice and Mushroom Savoury

Cooking container: 8" shallow round dish
Cooking time: 10 minutes
Number of servings: 4

4 plaice fillets
4 oz. (100 g) mushrooms
1 onion, sliced
2 tablespoons (30 ml) flour
¼ pint (150 ml) cream
¼ pint (150 ml) milk
4 oz. (100 g) grated cheese

Place the sliced onion and mushroom stalks in a dish with one tablespoon of butter and cook for [a] 2 minutes until tender. Remove and thoroughly drain onion and mushroom stalks and stir the flour into the butter. Add a further tablespoon of butter, cream and milk and stir well. Whisk before cooking for a further [b] minute. Remove from the oven and whisk again until thick. Add cheese, stir and replace in oven for [c] 1 minute. Whisk until thick again. Spread onion and mushroom stalks over the plaice fillets and spoon a little sauce mixture over them. Roll each fillet and secure with a wooden cocktail stick. Place the mushroom tops on the rolled fillets. Put the fillets in a dish and cover well with the remaining sauce. Cook for [c] 5-6 minutes. Before serving remove sticks and garnish with chopped parsley.

	500 watt		650 watt/2 power
a	3 minutes	a	2 minutes
b	1½ minutes	b	1 minute
c	2 minutes	c	1 minutes
d	7-8 minutes	d	4-5 minutes

	650 watt
a	PL.7 for 2½ minutes
b	PL.7 for 1½ minutes
c	PL.7 for 1½ minutes
d	PL.9 for 4-5 minutes

Cod with Herb Sauce

Cooking container: Shallow dish
Cooking time: 12 minutes
Number of servings: 4

4 cod or haddock steaks
8 oz. (225 g) frozen mixed vegetables
salt and pepper
10½ oz. (298 g) can condensed cream of celery soup,
undiluted
2 tablespoons (30 ml) milk
1 tablespoon (15 ml) fresh parsley, chopped
1 teaspoon (5 ml) fresh thyme, chopped
1 teaspoon (5 ml) fresh tarragon, chopped
1 teaspoon (5 ml) grated lemon rind

Place the cod into a fairly shallow dish. Surround with
vegetables. Combine all other ingredients — pour over
fish. Cook covered in oven for [a] 12 minutes — stand for
3 minutes before serving.

500 watt		650 watt/2 power	
a	15 minutes	a	10 minutes
650 watt			
a	PL.9 for 10 minutes		

Baked Stuffed Mackerel

Cooking container: Large shallow dish
Cooking time: 11-15 minutes
Number of servings: 4

4 mackerel, cleaned and gutted
1 apple, grated
3 oz. (75 g) white breadcrumbs
10½ oz. (298 g) condensed cream of mushroom soup,
undiluted
salt and pepper
½ soup can water

Combine apple, breadcrumbs, half of the soup and
seasoning. Use this to stuff the fish. Place the fish into a
shallow dish large enough to hold all the fish. Mix the
remaining soup with the water and pour over fish. Cover
and cook in oven for [a] 11-15 minutes (depending on
size of fish). Stand for 5 minutes before serving.

500 watt		650 watt/2 power	
a	15-18 minutes	a	10-14 minutes
650 watt			
a	PL.9 for 11-15 minutes		

Baked Trout and Bacon

Cooking container: Shallow dish
Cooking time: 14 minutes
Number of servings: 4

4 trout
8 oz. (225 g) streaky bacon
½ oz. (15 g) parsley
salt and pepper
lemon wedges

Line a shallow dish with two thirds of bacon. Lay trout
on top. Finely chop remaining bacon and scatter over
trout. Season with salt and pepper and sprinkle with
chopped parsley. Cook for approximately [a] 14 minutes
or until trout is cooked (timings will vary slightly
depending on the size of trout used). Serve with peas and
potatoes.
Suitable for freezing.

500 watt		650 watt/2 power	
a	16 minutes	a	12 minutes approx.
650 watt			
a	PL.9 for 12 minutes approx.		

Trout ready for cooking

95

Smoked Haddock

Cooking container: Shallow dish
Cooking time: 4 minutes   Number of servings: 1

8 oz. (225 g) smoked haddock
½ oz. (15 g) butter
2 tablespoons (30 ml) milk

Grease dish lightly, place the fish into it, pour over the milk and dot with butter. Cook covered in the microwave oven for [a] 4 minutes. Remove, cover and serve. This timing will alter slightly depending on the temperature and shape of the fish.

500 watt		650 watt/2 power	
a	5 minutes	a	3½ minutes
650 watt			
a	PL.9 for 3½ minutes		

Haddock with Prawns   *See colour plate page 97*

Cooking container: 3 pint casserole
Cooking time: 19 minutes   Number of servings: 4

4 pieces of haddock
4 oz. (100 g) prawns, peeled
½ pint (275 ml) water
1 oz. (25 g) butter
1 red pepper sliced
6 oz. (175 g) sliced mushrooms
1 medium onion chopped
seasoning

11½ oz. (326 g) can sweetcorn

Skin the haddock, place the skin in the water and heat in the oven for [a] 5 minutes. Leave to stand. Heat the butter for [b] 1 minute and add the onions, pepper and mushrooms. Sauté in the oven for [c] 5 minutes. Stir once during this cycle. Drain the fish skin from the water. Add the water and seasoning to the vegetables and lay the fish on top. Cover and cook for [d] 5 minutes. Add to the fish and prawns and sweetcorn. Cover and cook for a further [e] 3 minutes. Serve hot, garnished with parsley.

500 watt		650 watt/2 power	
a	6 minutes	a	5 minutes
b	1 minute	b	30 seconds
c	6 minutes	c	4½ minutes
d	6 minutes	d	4½ minutes
e	3 minutes	e	3 minutes
650 watt			
a	PL.9 for 5 minutes		
b	PL.7 for 1 minute		
c	PL.7 for 5 minutes		
d	PL.9 for 4½ minutes		
e	PL.8 for 3 minutes		

Trout Rosé

Cooking container: Shallow dish
Cooking time: 11 minutes
Number of servings: 2

2 medium trout, cleaned
1 oz. (25 g) butter
½ small onion, finely chopped
¼ pint (150 ml) rose wine
2 tablespoons (30 ml) hollandaise sauce
salt and pepper
croutons
parsley

Place trout in a shallow dish. Add the wine, sprinkle with the onions and dot with butter. Cook covered in the oven for [a] 5-6 minutes. Remove the trout from the stock. Skin the fish carefully. Heat the stock for [b] 3 minutes, add 3 tablespoons to the hollandaise sauce (which can be found in the sauce section) and mix well. Return the trout to the oven for [c] 2 minutes. Pour the sauce over the trout and heat for a further [d] 1 minute. Garnish with the croutons and parsley.

500 watt		650 watt/2 power	
a	6-7 minutes	a	4-5 minutes
b	4 minutes	b	2½ minutes
c	3 minutes	c	2 minutes
d	2 minutes	d	1 minute
650 watt			
a	PL.9 for 4-5 minutes		
b	PL.8 for 2½ minutes		
c	PL.8 for 2 minutes		
d	PL.8 for 1 minute		

Haddock with Prawns P.97

Crispy Cod

Cooking container: Shallow dish
Cooking time: 9 minutes
Number of servings: 2

2 cod cutlets
¾ oz. (20 g) butter
salt and pepper
2 rashers bacon
small handful of potato crisps

Place the cod cutlets on a dish, dot with the butter and sprinkle with the seasoning. Cover and cook in the oven for [a] 4 minutes. Remove cover and baste with the juices made during cooking. Return to the oven covered for a further [b] 2 minutes. Remove from the oven and stand to one side covered. Cook the bacon on absorbent paper in the oven for [c] 2-3 minutes until crisp. Crumble the bacon over the fish and sprinkle with the crushed potato crisps. If this dish is made in advance to be heated later, heat uncovered so that the bacon and crisps stay firm.

	500 watt		650 watt/2 power
a	5 minutes	a	3-4 minutes
b	2 minutes	b	1½ minutes
c	3-4 minutes	c	2 minutes

	650 watt
a	PL.9 for 3-4 minutes
b	PL.9 for 1½ minutes
c	PL.9 for 2 minutes

Kippers

Red Mullet with Tomatoes

Cooking container: Shallow dish
Cooking time: 10½ minutes
Number of servings: 2

2 red mullets, cleaned
½ medium onion, finely chopped
small tin tomatoes
garlic salt
½ oz. (15 g) butter
black pepper
1 teaspoon (5 ml) lemon juice
chopped parsley

Melt the butter in the oven for [a] 1 minute, sauté the onions in the butter for [b] 2½ minutes. Place the fish on top of the onions and cover with the tomatoes, lemon juice and a sprinkle of garlic salt. Cover and cook for [c] 7-8 minutes. Before serving, sprinkle with the chopped parsley. This dish can be served either hot or cold.

	500 watt		650 watt/2 power
a	1 minute	a	30 seconds
b	3½ minutes	b	2½ minutes
c	9 minutes	c	6-7 minutes

	650 watt
a	PL.8 for 45 seconds
b	PL.8 for 2½ minutes
c	PL.9 for 6-7 minutes

Pesce alla Florentina

Cooking container: Shallow round serving dish
Cooking time: 9 minutes
Number of servings: 4

1 lb (450 g) plaice fillets
½ pint (275 ml) milk
4 oz. (100 g) grated parmesan cheese
1 tablespoon (15 ml) flour
1½ oz. (40 g) butter
12 oz. (350 g) cooked weight of spinach

Place drained spinach into base of serving dish. Roll up plaice fillets and cook in separate dish for [a] 2 minutes. Place fillets onto spinach. In bowl melt butter, stir in flour, milk and liquid from fish. Heat for [b] 2 minutes then stir in cheese. Pour over fish. Cook for [c] 5 minutes or until fish is cooked.

	500 watt		650 watt/2 power
a	3 minutes	a	1½ minutes
b	3 minutes	b	1½ minutes
c	7 minutes	c	4½-5 minutes

	650 watt
a	PL.7 for 2 minutes
b	PL.9. for 1½ minutes
c	PL.8 for 5 minutes

Somerset Baked Cod

Cooking container: Covered dish and 2 pint bowl
Cooking time: 21 minutes   Number of servings: 4

4 cod steaks
salt and pepper
½ pint (275 ml) dry cider
Bouquet garni
1½ oz. (40 g) butter
1 onion, chopped
1½ oz. (40 g) flour
¼ pint (150 ml) milk
1 tablespoon (15 ml) chopped parsley
1 tablespoon (15 ml) lemon juice
12 oz. (300 g) mashed potato

Place fish, seasoning, cider and bouquet garni into dish — cover and cook in oven for [a] 12 minutes. In a 2 pint bowl cook onions with butter for [b] 3 minutes, add flour, stir well and cook for a further [c] 2 minutes. Drain the liquid from fish and add to milk to make ¾ pint. Add liquid to onion and flour, stir well and cook for [d] 4 minutes, stirring once during cooking cycle. Add the parsley and lemon, check seasoning and pour over fish. Serve with mashed potato piped around the fish.

	500 watt		650 watt/2 power
a	12 minutes	a	10 minutes
b	4 minutes	b	2½ minutes
c	2 minutes	c	2 minute
d	4-5 minutes	d	3½ minutes
	650 watt		
a	PL.9 for 10 minutes		
b	PL.7 for 3 minutes		
c	PL.7 for 2 minutes		
d	PL.7 for 4 minutes		

Salmon Layer Crisp

Cooking container: 2 pint bowl, 1½ pint shallow dish
Cooking time: 22¾ minutes   Number of servings: 3

1 x 7½ oz. (213 g) can salmon
1 oz. (25 g) butter
1 oz. (25 g) flour
½ pint (300 ml) milk including liquor from salmon
2 teaspoons (10 ml) lemon juice
1 egg yolk
seasoning
5 oz. (150 g) breadcrumbs
3 oz. (75 g) butter

Melt 1 oz. of butter in the oven for [a] 1 minute. Add the flour and mix well, then return to the oven for [b] 40 seconds. Heat the milk for [c] 2 minutes, gradually stir into the flour and mix until smooth. Return to the oven for [d] 2 minutes. Stir in the lemon juice, egg yolk, seasoning and flaked salmon. Cook for [e] 2 minutes. Stir and stand covered to one side. Heat the 3 oz. of butter in the oven for [f] 3 minutes. Mix in the breadcrumbs, heat for [g] 9 minutes, stirring with a fork several times or until brown. Stir on removal from oven. Place a layer of the breadcrumbs mix into a dish, cover with the salmon mix and top with the breadcrumbs. Heat in the oven for [h] 3 minutes.

	500 watt		650 watt/2 power
a	1 minute	a	30 seconds
b	1 minute	b	30 seconds
c	3 minutes	c	2 minutes
d	2 minutes	d	1½ minutes
e	3 minutes	e	2 minutes
f	3 minutes	f	1 minute
g	12 minutes	g	8 minutes
h	4 minutes	h	2½ minutes
	650 watt		
a	PL.8 for 45 seconds		
b	PL.8 for 45 seconds		
c	PL.8 for 2 minutes		
d	PL.8 for 2 minutes		
e	PL.9 for 2 minutes		
f	PL.9 for 2 minutes		
g	PL.7 for 11 minutes		
h	PL.8 for 3 minutes		

Trout Veloute with Grapes

Cooking container: Shallow dish
Cooking time: 11 minutes   Number of servings: 2

2 rainbow trout, thawed
4 tablespoons (60 ml) white wine
1 oz. (25 g) butter, melted
4 oz. (100 g) black grapes
6 green olives
salt and pepper
½ pint (275 ml) home-made or packet white sauce

Place trout into shallow dish. Add wine and seasoning. Brush with melted butter and cover with cling film. Cook for [a] 6 minutes (until cooked). Halve the grapes and remove pips. Slice the olives. Heat the sauce for [b] 3 minutes and add liquid from fish — season the sauce and add the grapes and olives. Cover fish with sauce and heat in oven for [c] 2 minutes.

Note: Make sauce before cooking fish so that it can just be heated before pouring over fish.

	500 watt		650 watt/2 power
a	7 minutes	a	5 minutes
b	3-4 minutes	b	2½ minutes
c	2½-3 minutes	c	2 minutes
	650 watt		
a	PL.9 for 5½ minutes		
b	PL.8 for 3¾ minutes		
c	PL.8 for 2 minutes		

Sweet & Sour Prawns

Cooking container: 3 pint casserole dish
Cooking time: 15 minutes
Number of servings: 4

2 teaspoons (10 ml) soy sauce
2 flat tablespoons (30 ml) cornflour
3 tablespoons (45 ml) soft dark-brown sugar
½ teaspoon (2.5 ml) ginger
1 teaspoon (5 ml) paprika
3 tablespoons (45 ml) vinegar
1 can pineapple pieces
2 teaspoons (10 ml) redcurrant jelly
8 oz. (225 g) prawns
1 small onion, chopped
1 green pepper, thinly sliced
1 carrot, cut into thin strips
4 tablespoons (60 ml) water

In a casserole dish combine the soy sauce, cornflour, sugar, ginger, paprika, vinegar, juice from the pineapple, redcurrant jelly and water. Place in the oven and heat for [a] 3 minutes. Stir well then add the carrots, onion and peppers. Cover and cook for [b] 6 minutes. Stir once during this cycle. Add the prawns and pineapple pieces, cover and heat for a further [c] 5 minutes. Stir well before serving.

	500 watt		650 watt/2 power
a	4 minutes	a	3 minutes
b	7 minutes	b	5 minutes
c	6 minutes	c	4 minutes

	650 watt
a	PL.7 for 5 minutes
b	PL.9 for 5 minutes
c	PL.8 for 4 minutes

Fish Pie

Cooking container: Casserole dish
Cooking time: 16½ minutes
Number of servings: 4

1 lb (450 g) fish
½ pint (300 ml) milk
2 hard-boiled eggs
1 oz. (25 g) butter
1 oz. (25 g) flour
½ teaspoon (2.5 ml) celery salt
pepper
chopped parsley
1 lb (450 g) mashed potatoes

Cook the fish covered in the oven for [a] 5 minutes. Remove and stand to one side. Melt the butter in the oven for [b] 1 minute. Stir in the flour and cook for [c] 40 seconds. Heat the milk for [d] 2 minutes and gradually add to the flour, stirring well. Return to the oven for [e] 1½ minutes. Mix well. Flake the fish and add with the seasoning, parsley and chopped hard-boiled eggs to the milk. Line a dish with the mashed potatoes, pour the fish into the centre and heat for [f] 6 minutes in the oven. Remove from oven and place under the grill to brown just before serving.

	500 watt		650 watt/2 power
a	6 minutes	a	4 minutes
b	1 minute	b	30 seconds
c	1 minute	c	30 seconds
d	3 minutes	d	2 minutes
e	2 minutes	e	1½ minutes
f	8 minutes	f	5 minutes

	650 watt
a	PL.9 for 4 minutes
b	PL.7 for 1 minute
c	PL.7 for 1 minute
d	PL.9 for 2 minutes
e	PL.7 for 1½ minutes
f	PL.8 for 6 minutes

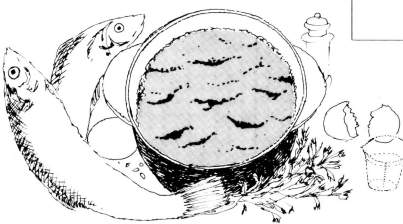

Vegetables

Vegetables

Cooking of vegetables in the microwave oven is easy, and when you see the lovely colour the vegetables keep and taste the flavour you will always choose this method for cooking them.

As a general rule:

1 Try to cut the vegetables as even in size as possible.
2 Cook vegetables in serving dish with a little water as directed.
3 Always cover vegetables when cooking in the microwave oven.
4 Do not add salt to the vegetables until after they have been cooked as this can lead to dehydration of the vegetables and overcooking.
5 Always stand covered before serving.

Microwave method — Frozen vegetables:

To cook peas and sweetcorn, these can be cooked in the oven with no extra water as long as the dish is covered.
1 Place the frozen peas into a serving dish, add a knob of butter, cover and cook for the time recommended.

All other frozen vegetables should be cooked in the following way:

1 Place into container.
2 Add recommended amount of water.
3 Cover container and cook in microwave oven for recommended time.
4 Stand covered for suggested time before draining and seasoning.

Microwave method — Fresh vegetables:
Cook fresh vegetables by the following method:

1 Place clean prepared vegetables into serving dish. Add required amount of water, cover and cook in the oven for recommended time.
2 On removal from the oven, the vegetables should be left to stand for recommended time before eating.
3 If vegetables have been cooked in advance of the meal, then they can be reheated. Vegetables are best reheated with a knob of butter.
4 Remember to season the vegetables lightly when they come out of the oven after draining.

Large amounts of vegetables to be cooked in the microwave oven will take the same time or longer than when cooked in the conventional way, but the flavour and colour certainly recompense this.

Preparation of Broccoli

Preparation of Broad Beans

Frozen Vegetable Chart

1. All amounts are 1 lb unless stated.
2. All vegetables should be covered unless stated.
3. Less weight of vegetables will take less time.
4. All timings on 650 watt oven are on power level 9 or full power.
5. All timings are approximate dependings on quality, size and container used.
6. All timings are approximate mins per lb. (450g)

Vegetables	Water added	500 watt	600 watt	650 watt	Standing time
Asparagus	4 tablespoons	19	17	15	5
Broad Beans	6 tablespoons	18	15	14	5
Broccoli 8 oz.	4 tablespoons	15	12	10	7
Brussels Sprouts	4 tablespoons	17	14	12	5
Cabbage	6 tablespoons	17	14	12	3
Carrots (Baby)	4 tablespoons	19	16	15	7
Carrots (Sliced)	4 tablespoons	17	15	13	5
Cauliflower florets	2 tablespoons	17	14	12	7
Courgettes	2 tablespoons	16	14	12	5
Leeks	2 tablespoons	19	17	15	5
Mixed Vegetables	2 tablespoons	14	12	10	5
Mushrooms	knob of butter	14	12	10	3
Onions, (Sliced)	4 tablespoons	16	14	12	5
Parsnips	6 tablespoons	19	17	15	7
Peas	knob of butter	14	12	10	5
Salsify	5 tablespoons 1 tablespoon lemon juice	18	15	13	3
Sliced Beans	6 tablespoons	16	14	12	5
Spinach		14	12	10	5
Sweetcorn	4 tablespoons	16	14	12	5

Oven chips/grill chips.
Place 6 oz. of chips spread out on a plate into oven. Heat
3 minutes on full power. Shake plate and heat for a
further 2-3 minutes. The chips can also be heated on a
preheated browning dish, for 3-4 minutes.

Fresh Vegetable Chart

1 All amounts are 1 lb unless stated.
2 All vegetables should be covered unless stated.
3 Smaller quantities vegetables will take less time.
4 All timings on 650 watt oven are on power level 9. or full power.
5 All timings are approximate dependings on quality, size and container used.
6 All timings are approximate mins per lb. (450g)

Vegetable	Preparation	Water added	500 watt	600 watt	650 watt	Standing time
Artichoke 8 oz.	Wash then shake off excess water. Wrap in cling film.		10	8	4	4
Asparagus		2 tablespoons	12	10	8	5
Bean Sprouts 12 oz.		1 oz. butter	6	5	3	2
Beetroot	Cut in half	4 tablespoons	13	11	9	10
Broad Beans	Shell	4 tablespoons	15	12	10	5
Broccoli 8 oz.	Slice lengthways	4 tablespoons	12-15	10-12	8-9	5
Carrots	Slice thinly	4 tablespoons	12	12	10	5
Cauliflower Florets	Separate	4 tablespoons	14	12	10	10
Cauliflower	Trim outer leaves	6 tablespoons	16	13	11	5
Celery	Cut 2½'' lengthways	3 tablespoons	18	15	10-12	5
Courgettes	Slice	knob of butter	15	13	11	5
Fennel	Slice thinly	1 tablespoon	15	12-13	11-12	10
Leeks	Slice 1'' size	4 tablespoons	12	10	8	5
Button Mushrooms 8 oz.	Wash	1 oz. butter	6	5	4	2
Marrow	Cut in cubes	knob of butter	12	10	8	5
New Potatoes	Cut into small size	6 tablespoons	15	12	8-10	5
Onions, small	Leave whole	2 tablespoons	12	10	8	10
Parsnips	Slice thinly 2'' in length	4 tablespoons	15	12	10	10
Peas	Shell	knob of butter	14	12	10	5
Runner Beans	String & Slice	4 tablespoons	15	12	10	5
Spring Cabbage	Wash & shred	2 tablespoons	13	11	9	10
Sprouts	Remove outer leaves	4 tablespoons	13	11	9	5
Swede	Dice	4 tablespoons	20	18	16	10
Tomatoes 8 oz.	Halved	Brush melted butter	5	4	3	10

Blanching

Blanching Vegetables in the Microwave Oven

First of all it should be borne in mind that if large quantities of vegetables are to be blanched at any one time, then conventional blanching will be quicker and easier.

However, microwave blanching does assist in the retention of nutrients, especially absorbic acid, which are lost to a greater extent in conventional water blanching. Prepare vegetables in the usual way and blanch only 1 lb (450 g) at a time. Two methods can be used:-

1   After preparing vegetables, rinse in clean water, place in a boil-a-bag and tie loosely with string (there is no need for the addition of water). Blanch for half the recommended time, turn the bag over and blanch for the remainder of the time. Plunge imediately into ice cold water (the bag will tend to float so keep it under water and make sure that water does not enter the neck of the bag). Dry the bag and freeze. The advantage of this method is that vegetables can be blanched, cooled, frozen, and re-heated in the same bag.

2   Place the vegetables in a suitable dish and add approximately 3 fl. oz. water. Cover with lid or cling film (remember to pierce film to allow air to escape). Blanch for half recommended time, stir and continue to blanch for remainder of time. Plunge immediately into ice cold water until cool, drain, dry, pack and freeze.

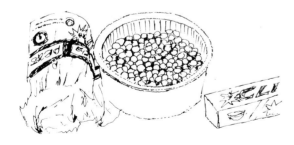

(We have been doing some work on blanching and cooking vegetables in normal freezer bags, and have been successful with 200 g and 300 g bags, but would not recommend using 120 g polythene bags, which should only be used for defrosting items in the microwave oven.)

Timings and information supplied courtesy of Lakeland Plastics Ltd.

Vegetable	Blanching	Time (650 watt)
Asparagus	Small stalks	2 mins
	Medium stalks	2½ mins
	Large stalks	3 mins
Aubergine	½" slices	2 mins
Beans — French	Whole beans	2½ mins
and Runner	Cut beans	2 mins
	Sliced beans	1½ mins
Broad Beans		2 mins
Broccoli	Thin stalks	2 mins
	Mediums stalks	2½ mins
	Thick stalks	3-3½ mins
Brussels	Small	2½ mins
Sprouts	Medium	3 mins
	Large	3-3½ mins
Cabbage		2 mins
Capsicum	Halves or Slices	2 mins
Carrots		3 mins
Cauliflower	Florets	2½ mins
Celery	Pieces	3 mins
	Hearts	4 mins
Corn-on-cob	Small	3 mins
	Medium	4 mins
	Large	5 mins
Courgettes	½" Slices	1½ mins
	or Small whole	(boil-a-bag method recommended) Sauté in butter 1 min
Globe	Whole	4 mins
Artichokes	Hearts	3 mins
Jerusalem		
Artichokes	Slices	2½ mins
Kale		3 mins
Leeks	Slices	2 mins
	Whole	3 mins
Mushrooms		Sauté in butter 1 min
Onions	Small whole	3 mins
Parsnips		
Turnips		3 mins
(Swedes)		
Peas	Small	1½ mins
	Medium	2 mins
Spinach		1½ mins
Sweet Corn		2½ mins
Kernals		

Glazed Beetroot

Cooking container: Browning dish
Cooking time: 4 minutes
Number of servings: 2-3

½ oz. (15 g) butter
½ teaspoon (2.5 ml) sugar
8 oz. (225 g) cooked beetroot (small whole)
½ lemon, grated
salt and pepper
1 teaspoon (5 ml) lemon juice
2 teaspoons (10 ml) capers

Heat browning dish for [a] 4 minutes in microwave oven. Add butter and stir in sugar and lemon rind. Toss the beetroot in this mixture, cook for [b] 1 minute, stir and then cook for a further [c] minute. Add the lemon juice, seasoning and capers, cook for a further [d] 2 minutes before serving sprinkled with parsley.

	500 watt		650 watt/2 power
a	5 minutes	a	4 minutes
b	1 minute	b	45 seconds
c	2 minutes	c	1 minute
d	3 minutes	d	2 minutes
	650 watt		
a	PL.8 for 4 minutes		
b	PL.8 for 1 minute		
c	PL.8 for 1 minute		
d	PL.8 for 2 minutes		

Creamed Broad Beans

Cooking container: 1½ pint casserole
Cooking time: 14 minutes
Number of servings: 2-3

8 oz. (225 g) broad beans
½ oz. (10 g) butter
1 small onion, chopped
3 rashers streaky bacon, chopped
2 tablespoons (30 ml) cream
salt and pepper

Cook the beans in a 1½ pint casserole covered with 4 tablespoons of water for [a] 9 minutes. Drain then season lightly and leave to stand covered. Cook the bacon and onions in the butter for [b] 5 minutes. Stir into beans with cream. If reheating, reheat carefully before serving.

	500 watt		650 watt/2 power
a	11-12 minutes	a	8 minutes
b	6 minutes	b	4½-5 minutes
	650 watt		
a	PL.9 for 8 minutes		
b	PL.7 for 5 minutes		

Broad Beans in Tomato Sauce

Cooking container: 2 pint casserole
Cooking time: 7½ minutes
Number of servings: 4

12 oz. (350 g) cooked broad beans
1 tablespoon (15 ml) oil
1 small onion, finely chopped
small can tomatoes
1 teaspoon (5 ml) tomato pureé
2 tablespoons (30 ml) water
¼ teaspoon (1.25 ml) sugar
salt and pepper

Melt the oil in the oven for [a] 30 seconds, sauté the onion for [b] 2 minutes, add all other ingredients and cook for [c] 2 minutes covered. Stir well and return to the oven for [d] 1 minute uncovered. Pour over the broad beans and heat in the oven covered for [e] 2 minutes.

	500 watt		650 watt/2 power
a	45 seconds	a	30 seconds
b	3 minutes	b	2 minutes
c	3½ minutes	c	1½ minutes
d	1 minute	d	1 minute
e	3 minutes	e	1½ minutes
	650 watt		
a	PL.7 for 30 seconds		
b	PL.7 for 2 minutes		
c	PL.7 for 2 minutes		
d	PL.7 for 1 minute		
e	PL.8 for 1¾ minutes		

Pepperonata

Cooking container: 2 pint casserole
Cooking time: 23 minutes
Number of servings: 4-6

2 tablespoons (30 ml) oil
4 sliced green peppers
4 sliced sticks of celery
1 large onion, sliced
1 clove garlic, crushed
10½ oz. (295 g) condensed cream of tomato soup — undiluted
salt and pepper

Combine oil, garlic, onions, celery and peppers. Place covered in oven for [a] 8 minutes. Add all other ingredients and cook uncovered for [b] 15 minutes.

	500 watt		650 watt/2 power
a	10 minutes	a	7½ minutes
b	20 minutes	b	14 minutes
	650 watt		
a	PL.8 for 7½ minutes		
b	PL.8 for 15 minutes		

Broccoli with Lemon Sauce

Cooking container: 2 pint bowl
Cooking time: 17 minutes
Number of servings: 3-4

1 oz. (25 g) butter
1 oz. (25 g) flour
½ pint (275 ml) chicken stock
2 egg yolks
2 tablespoons (30 ml) lemon juice
salt and pepper
1 packet broccoli spears

Unseal the packet of broccoli spears and place into the microwave oven and cook for [a] 10 minutes. Place into serving dish and leave covered. Melt butter in a 2 pint bowl. Stir in flour, cook for [b] 1 minute, add stock stirring well and cook for [c] 4½ minutes, stirring halfway through cooking cycle. Allow to cool and add egg yolks and lemon juice. Season to taste. Pour over broccoli and heat in oven for [d] 1½ minutes.

	500 watt		650 watt/2 power
a	12 minutes	a	9 minutes
b	1½ minutes	b	30 seconds
c	5½-6 minutes	c	4½ minutes
d	2½ minutes	d	1 minute

	650 watt
a	PL.9 for 9 minutes
b	PL.7 for 1 minute
c	PL.9 for 4½ minutes
d	PL.8 for 1½ minutes

Bavarian Red Cabbage & Buttered Mint Carrots

Bavarian Red Cabbage

Cooking container: 3 pint casserole
Cooking time: 30½ minutes
Number of servings: 4-6

12 oz. (350 g) red cabbage, finely shredded
1 large cooking apple, peeled and sliced
1 small onion stuck with cloves
2 tablespoons (30 ml) lemon juice
1 oz. (25 g) margarine
1 teaspoon (5 ml) cornflour
1 bayleaf
1 tablespoon (15 ml) sugar
pinch cinnamon
⅓ pint (200 ml) stock

Melt the margarine in the oven for [a] ½ minute. Toss the cabbage in the margarine. Cook for [b] 8 minutes. Add the onion, bayleaf, lemon juice, sugar and cinnamon. Stir and heat covered for [c] 5 minutes. Add the stock and apple. Cook covered for [d] 12 minutes. Remove the onion and bayleaf, mix the cornflour with a little water and stir into the cabbage. Cook covered for a further [e] 5 minutes. Stir before serving.

	500 watt		650 watt/2 power
a	1 minute	a	30 seconds
b	10 minutes	b	7 minutes
c	7 minutes	c	4½ minutes
d	14 minutes	d	10 minutes
e	5 minutes	e	4 minutes

	650 watt
a	PL.7 for 30 seconds
b	PL.7 for 8 minutes
c	PL.9 for 4½ minutes
d	PL.9 for 10 minutes
e	PL.9 for 4 minutes

Italian-style Cauliflower

See colour plate page 109

Cooking container: Large casserole dish
Cooking time: 25½-28½ minutes
Number of servings: 4-5

1 large cauliflower
2 teaspoons (10 ml) oil
1 onion sliced
4 stuffed olives sliced
14 oz. (397 g) can tomatoes
10½ oz. (298 g) can condensed cream of chicken soup, undiluted
3 tablespoons (45 ml) milk
2 oz. (50 g) grated cheese
good pinch garlic
good pinch marjoram
salt and pepper

Prepare cauliflower for cooking. Keep whole and place with 4 tablespoons of water into a covered dish — cook for [a] 15-18 minutes (depending on size). Stand covered on removal from oven. Place onion with oil in oven for [b] 2 minutes, add tomatoes, marjoram, garlic and olives. Heat for [c] 5 minutes, stir and pour over cauliflower. Combine soup and milk — heat for [d] 1½ minutes — stir and pour over cauliflower. Sprinkle with cheese and return the dish to oven for [e] 2 minutes.

	500 watt		650 watt/2 power
a	18-20 minutes	a	12-15 minutes
b	3 minutes	b	2 minutes
c	6 minutes	c	4½ minutes
d	3 minutes	d	1 minute
e	3 minutes	e	2 minutes

	650 watt	
a	PL.9 for 12-15 minutes
b	PL.7 for 2 minutes
c	PL.9 for 4½ minutes
d	PL.8 for 1½ minutes
e	PL.8 for 2 minutes

Cauliflower Polonaise

Cooking container: 3 pint dish
Cooking time: 16½ minutes
Number of servings: 4-6

1 medium sized cauliflower
1 hard boiled egg
1 oz. (25 g) butter
1 oz. (25 g) breadcrumbs
seasoning

Cook the cauliflower with 8 tablespoons of water for [a] 13 minutes (depending on size) in a covered 3 pint dish. Drain, season and keep covered. Chop finely the white of the egg and rub the yolk through a sieve. Melt the butter in the oven for [b] ½ minute, toss in the breadcrumbs and cook until brown, approximately [c] 3 minutes. Stir every minute. Garnish the cauliflower with the breadcrumbs, egg white and yolk before serving.

	500 watt		650 watt/2 power
a	14 minutes	a	12 minutes
b	1 minute	b	30 seconds
c	Approx. 4 minutes	c	Approx. 2½ minutes

	650 watt	
a	PL.9 for 12 minutes
b	PL.7 for 45 seconds
c	PL.7 for approx. 3 minutes

Crunchy Brussels Sprouts

Cooking container: 2 pint bowl
Cooking time: 14 minutes
Number of servings: 3-4

8 oz. (225 g) brussels sprouts
1 oz. (25 g) butter
1 small onion, peeled and finely chopped
2 oz. (50 g) coarsely chopped blanched almonds
salt and black pepper

Cook the brussels sprouts with 2 tablespoons of water covered for [a] 8 minutes, drain and season, keep covered. Place the butter, almonds and onion into a 2 pint bowl and cook for [b] 6 minutes. Shake the bowl twice during cooking cycle. Spoon mixture over the brussels sprouts and serve.

	500 watt		650 watt/2 power
a	10 minutes	a	7 minutes
b	8 minutes	b	5½ minutes

	650 watt	
a	PL.9 for 7 minutes
b	PL.9 for 5½ minutes

Italian Style Cauliflower P.109

Courgettes in Tomato Sauce

Cooking container: 3 pint casserole
Cooking time: 19 minutes
Number of servings: 6-8

2 lb (900 g) courgettes cut into ½" rings
¼ pint (150 ml) water
¼ pint (150 ml) dry white wine
1 onion, peeled and finely chopped
1 clove of garlic peeled and crushed
2 tablespoons (30 ml) tomato puree
¾ teaspoon (1.5 ml) mixed herbs
1 bay leaf

Place all ingredients except courgettes into a 3 pint bowl and cook for [a] 7 minutes, stirring once during cycle. Add courgettes, cover and cook for [b] 12-15 minutes or until the courgettes are tender, stir once during cycle. Leave to stand covered for 5 minutes.

	500 watt		650 watt/2 power
a	8 minutes	a	6½ minutes
b	18-20 minutes stirring twice	b	12-15 minutes

	650 watt	
	a	PL.8 for 7 minutes
	b	PL.9 for 12-15 minutes

Mushrooms & Peas

Cooking container: 2½ pint casserole
Cooking time: 11 minutes
Number of servings: 4-5

8 oz (225 g) small button mushrooms
8 oz (225 g) frozen peas
4 spring onions finely chopped
1½ oz (40 g) butter

Heat the butter in casserole for [a] 1 minute. Add the spring onions and cook covered for [b] 2 minutes. Add the mushrooms, coat in butter, cover and cook for [c] 2 minutes. Stand covered. Cook peas covered for [d] 6 minutes, drain and serve combined with mushrooms.

	500 watt		650 watt/2 power
a	1½ minutes	a	30 seconds
b	2½ minutes	b	1½ minutes
c	3 minutes	c	1½ minutes
d	7 minutes	d	5 minutes

	650 watt	
	a	PL.9 for 45 seconds
	b	PL.9 for 1½ minutes
	c	PL.9 for 1½ minutes
	d	PL.9 for 5 minutes

Stuffed Tomatoes

Cooking container: Plate
Cooking time: 10½ minutes
Number of servings: 4

4 large tomatoes
1 small onion, finely chopped
2 oz. (50 g) bacon, finely chopped
1½ oz. (40 g) breadcrumbs
1 oz. (25 g) butter
salt and pepper

Cut the top off the tomatoes, scoop out the inside and chop. Heat the butter in the oven for [a] 45 seconds. Add the onion and bacon, and sauté for [b] 2½ minutes. Add the breadcrumbs, seasoning and tomato flesh, stir and heat for [c] 2 minutes. Fill the tomatoes and cover with the tops. Cook in the oven for [d] 5 minutes. Stand for 1 minute before serving.

	500 watt		650 watt/2 power
a	1 minute	a	30 seconds
b	4 minutes	b	2 minutes
c	3 minutes	c	1 minute
d	6 minutes	d	4 minutes

	650 watt	
	a	PL.7 for 1 minute
	b	PL.7 for 2½ minutes
	c	PL.9 for 1 minute
	d	PL.9 for 4 minutes

Braised Celery

Cooking container: Round baker
Cooking time: 20 minutes
Number of servings: 4

1 head of celery, cleaned and cut into 2" pieces
½ pint (275 ml) chicken stock
butter

Lightly grease a round baker. Add in the celery and the stock. Cover with cling film and cook in the oven for [a] 20 minutes. This will depend of course on the size of the celery.

	500 watt		650 watt/2 power
a	23-24 minutes	a	16-18 minutes

	650 watt	
	a	PL.9 for 18 minutes

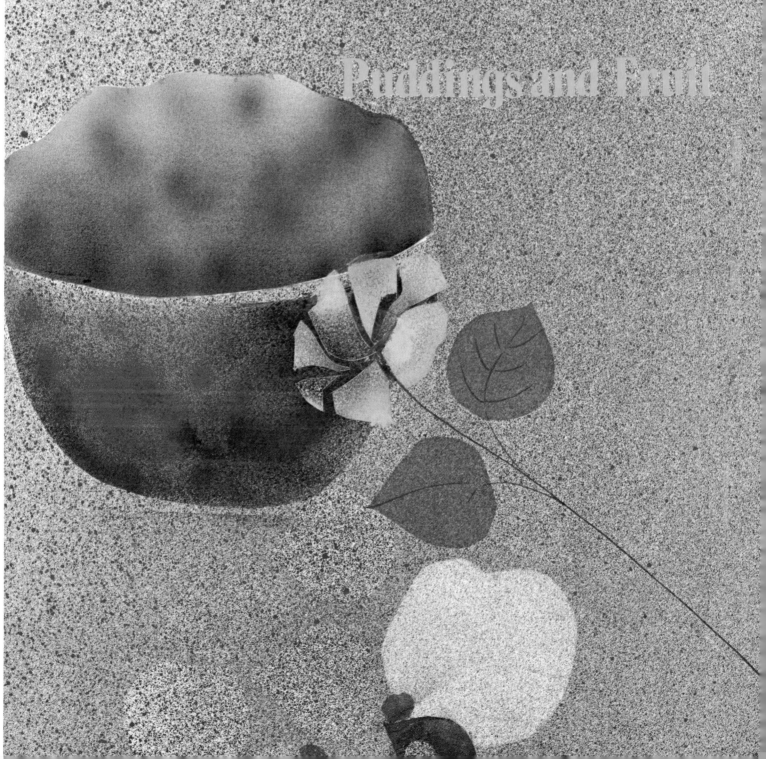

Puddings and Fruit

Baked Apples

Cooking container: Round baker
Cooking time: 11 minutes
Number of servings: 4

4 cooking apples, cored, total weight approx 2 lb.
4 tablespoons (60 ml) demerara sugar
1 oz. (25 g) butter
2 tablespoons (30 ml) sweet cider

For the Sauce

2 level tablespoons (30 ml) demerara sugar
¼ pint (150 ml) cider
flaked almonds

Place the apples in a shallow dish, fill each with 1 tablespoon of sugar and top with ¼ oz. butter. Pour 2 tablespoons of cider into the base of the dish. Cover and cook in the oven for [a] 6-6½ minutes, depending on the type of apple. Remove the apples from the syrup. Make up the syrup to 5 fl. oz. with the additional cider. Heat the syrup with the sugar in the oven for [b] 5 minutes. Stir twice carefully during this cycle. Pour the syrup over the apples, garnish with the almonds and serve.

	500 watt		650 watt/2 power
a	7-9 minutes (turn once)	a	6-6½ minutes
b	6 minutes	b	4½-5 minutes
650 watt			
a	PL.9 for 6-6½ minutes		
b	PL.7 for 5-5½ minutes		

Banana Treat

Cooking container: Round baker
Cooking time: 3 minutes
Number of servings: 2

2 bananas, peeled and sliced
½ oz. (15 g) butter
juice of one orange
pinch of cinnamon

Heat the butter, orange juice and cinnamon together for [a] 1¼ minutes. Stir in banana and heat for a further [b] 1¾ minutes. Sprinkle with chopped walnuts and serve.

	500 watt		650 watt/2 power
a	2½ minutes	a	1 minute
b	2 minutes	b	1½ minutes
650 watt			
a	PL.9 for 1 minute		
b	PL.9 for 1½ minutes		

Ruby Pears

Cooking container: 2½ pint casserole dish
Cooking time: 9 minutes
Number of servings: 4

4 well shaped ripe pears — peeled
5 fl. oz. (142 ml) water
5 oz. (150 g) sugar
1 lemon (juice and grated rind)
4 cloves
red food colouring

Heat sugar and water for about [a] 4 minutes. Stir to ensure that sugar is dissolved. Add pears, lemon juice, grated lemon rind and cloves and cook for [b] 5 minutes. Spoon the syrup over the pears once during cooking. Carefully remove pears. Add red colouring to syrup for bright pink colouring. Return pears to syrup and turn frequently for even colour. Serve hot or cold with cream.

	500 watt		650 watt/2 power
a	5 minutes	a	3 minutes
b	5½ minutes	b	4 minutes
650 watt			
a	PL.7 for 4 minutes		
b	PL.9 for 4 minutes		

Ruby Pears

Cherry Crumble

Cooking container: 2½ pint casserole
Cooking time: 22 minutes
Number of servings: 4-5

1 lb (450 g) pitted cherries
¼ pint (150 ml) water
2 oz. (50 g) caster sugar
2 teaspoons (10 ml) cornflour
1 teaspoon (5 ml) lemon juice
2 oz. (50 g) margarine
4 oz. (100 g) plain flour
4 oz. (100 g) demerara sugar
½ teaspoon (2.5 ml) cinnamon

Keep 10 cherries for decoration. Place the cherries, sugar and water into a 3 pint bowl. Cook covered for [a] 9 minutes. Strain the cherries from the juice. Mix the cornflour with a little of the juice until smooth. Add the rest of the liquid and lemon juice. Cook for [b] 3 minutes. Add the cherries and place in a 2½ pint casserole. Rub margarine into flour, add cinnamon and sugar and sprinkle over cherries. Garnish with spare cherries and cook in oven for [c] 10 minutes.

	500 watt		650 watt/2 power
a	10 minutes	a	6 minutes
b	3 minutes	b	1-2 minutes
c	10 minutes (turn once)	c	7-8 minutes

	650 watt	
a	PL.9 for 6 minutes
b	PL.9 for 1-2 minutes
c	PL.8 for 6 minutes

Flaked Rice Pudding

Cooking container: 4 pint casserole dish
Cooking time: 19 minutes
Number of servings: 4-5

2 oz. (50 g) flaked rice
1 pint (550 ml) milk
1 oz. (25 g) caster sugar

Combine all ingredients into a 4 pint casserole dish. Place into the oven and cook for [a] 19 minutes. Stir twice during cycle and allow to stand for 5 minutes on removal from the oven.

	500 watt		650 watt/2 power
a	23-25 minutes	a	15-16 minutes

	650 watt
a	PL.8 for 14 minutes

Fruit Surprise

Fruit Surprise

Cooking container: 4 wine glasses
Cooking time: 3 minutes
Number of servings: 4

1 can fruit pie filling
1 egg white
1 tablespoon (15 ml) caster sugar
1 tablespoon (15 ml) sherry
chopped nut topping

Mix the pie filling with the sherry. Divide between 4 wine glasses. Whisk the egg white, fold in the caster sugar and pile this meringue onto the fruit filling. Heat in the oven for [a] 2-3 minutes (until meringue has expanded and fruit heated). Sprinkle with nuts and serve.

	500 watt		650 watt/2 power
a	2-3 minutes	a	1½-2 minutes

	650 watt
a	P.7 for 2-3 minutes

Lemon Meringue Pie

Cooking container: Flan dish
Cooking time: 6 minutes
Number of servings: 4

2 lemons, grated and squeezed
water
2 tablespoons (30 ml) cornflour
2 oz (50 g) butter
6 oz (175 g) caster sugar
2 eggs separated
1 biscuit flan case

Make the lemon juice up to half a pint with the water.
Blend the cornflour with the water, heat in the oven with
the grated rind, butter and 3 oz. of the sugar for [a] 2
minutes, stir and return to the oven for a further [b] 2
minutes. Stir well on removal. Allow to cool slightly and
add the egg yolks, mix well, heat for [c] 2 minutes in the
oven and pour the lemon mix into the flan case. Beat the
egg whites until stiff and fold in the remaining sugar. Pile
the meringue onto the lemon mix and place under the
grill to brown. Serve hot or cold.

	500 watt		650 watt/2 power
a	3 minutes	a	3 minutes
b	3 minutes	b	3 minutes
c	2½ minutes	c	1½ minutes

	650 watt	
a	PL.9 for 3 minutes	
b	PL.9 for 2 minutes	
c	PL.7 for 1 minute	

Christmas Pudding

Cooking container: 2 x 2 lb or
                    2½ lb basins OR
                    4 x 1 lb basins
Cooking time: 2-2½ lb = 14 minutes
             1 lb   = 8½ minutes
Number of servings: 6-8

6 oz (175 g) currants
4 oz (100 g) sultanas
10 oz (275 g) raisins
4 oz (100 g) dried mixed peel
4 tablespoons (60 ml) brandy
1 tablespoon (15 ml) black treacle
3 grade 3 eggs, lightly beaten
5 fl. oz (142 ml) milk
2 teaspoons (10 ml) gravy browning
4 oz (100 g) dark soft brown sugar
4 oz (100 g) caster sugar

6 oz (175 g) shredded suet
3 oz (75 g) fresh breadcrumbs
3 oz (75 g) chopped almonds
1 oz (25 g) glace cherries
½ level teaspoon (2.5 ml) salt
¼ level teaspoon (1.25 ml) cinnamon
¼ level teaspoon (1.25 ml) powdered ginger
¼ level teaspoon (1.25 ml) ground nutmeg
grated rind of ½ lemon
grated rind of ½ orange
6 oz (175 g) plain flour

Put dried peel, sultanas, raisins and currants in a large
bowl and cover with boiling water. Heat for [a] 4
minutes then leave to stand for 1 hour. Strain, put fruit
back in bowl, add brandy and leave to stand for several
hours, preferably overnight. Stir in all the liquids, mix
in all other ingredients. Grease basins and put mixture
into basins. Cover top loosely with cling film. Do not
insert any silver coins or charms.
Cook puddings separately.

2 lb pudding — Microwave 5 minutes
b (i)   Stand 4 minutes
               Microwave 5 minutes

1 lb pudding — Microwave 2 minutes
b (ii)   Stand 4 minutes
               Microwave 2½ minutes

	500 watt		650 watt/2 power
a	5 minutes	a	4 minutes
b (i)	6 minutes	b (i)	4½ minutes
	Stand 5 minutes		Stand 4 minutes
	6-7 minutes		4 minutes
b (ii)	3 minutes	b (ii)	1½ minutes
	Stand 4 minutes		Stand 4 minutes
	2½-3 minutes		2 minutes

	650 watt	
a	PL.9 for 4 minutes	
b (i)	PL.5 for 17 minutes	
b (ii)	PL.5 for 9 minutes	

When cold, wrap in cling film and aluminium foil and
store in a cool place. Reheat, preferably in slices, at
approx. 2 minutes to the pound weight.

Apricot Sponge

Cooking container: Round cake baker 8"
Cooking time: 7 minutes
Number of servings: 5-6

3½ oz. (85 g) butter
2 oz. (50 g) sifted icing sugar
2 oz. (50 g) sifted soft dark brown sugar
3 eggs (grade 4)
4 oz. (100 g) cornflour
4 oz. (100 g) self raising flour
1 teaspoon (5 ml) baking powder
3 tablespoons (45 ml) cold water

Filling: Apricot jam
        Small tin apricots

Covering: Whipped cream

Cream butter and sugars until fluffy. Add 3 well beaten eggs slowly and keep beating the mixture. Sift the cornflour, self raising flour and baking powder. Add slowly to the creamed mixture then add 3 tablespoons of cold water. Grease cake baker and put a greaseproof circle in the base. Cook for [a] 7 minutes. Take out of oven and shake the dish. Turn out onto a rack. Cut in half. On one half put apricot jam and sliced apricots. Put other half on top. Decorate all over with one of the suggested coverings. Decorate the top with apricots.

	500 watt		650 watt/2 power
a	8 minutes	a	5-5½ minutes
	650 watt		
	a	PL.9 for 5-5½ minutes	

French Apple Tart

Cooking container: Serving plate 8" flan case
Cooking time: 10½ minutes
Number of servings: 6

1 x 8" shallow cooked flan case
3 sweet eating apples, peeled, cored and finely sliced
12 oz. (350 g) cooking apples, peeled, cored and chopped
caster sugar
allspice
apricot jam
1 teaspoon (5 ml) arrowroot
2 teaspoons (10 ml) lemon juice

Place the flan case onto a serving plate. Cook the cooking apples, covered in the microwave oven for [a] 3-4 minutes (or until soft). Purée the apples, sweeten with the sugar to taste and add a pinch of allspice. Spread the stewed apples over the base of the flan and cover with the sliced apples to form an attractive pattern. Mix together the lemon juice, 2 tablespoons of water and 2 tablespoons of sieved apricot jam. Heat together in the microwave oven for [b] 1½ minutes. Stir and spread over the apples. Place the flan in the microwave oven and cook for [c] 5 minutes or until apples are soft but still keeping their shape. Sieve a further 2 tablespoons of the apricot jam adding 2 tablespoons of water and a teaspoon of arrowroot. Bring to boil in the microwave oven, stir and cool slightly. Spread this mix over the apples, allow to cool and serve as required with cream.

	500 watt		650 watt/2 power
a	4-5 minutes	a	4 minutes
b	2½ minutes	b	1 minute
c	7 minutes	c	4 minutes
	650 watt		
	a	PL.9 for 4 minutes	
	b	PL.7 for 2 minutes	
	c	PL.9 for 4 minutes	

Stuffed Peaches

Cooking container: Flat serving dish
Cooking time: 6¾ minutes
Number of servings: 3-6

3 good-sized ripe peaches
1 oz. (25 g) sponge cake crumbs
1 oz. (25 g) ground almonds
1 oz. (25 g) caster sugar
2 tablespoons (30 ml) medium dry sherry
demerara sugar

Place the sponge cake crumbs, ground almonds and caster sugar in a bowl. Add the sherry and mix well. Heat the whole peaches in the oven for [a] 45 seconds. Allow to cool and gently remove the skins. Cut the peaches in half, remove the stone and place in a shallow dish. Pile the stuffing into the stone cavities and sprinkle with the demerara sugar. Place in the oven uncovered and cook for [b] 6 minutes. Garnish with blanched almonds and cherries. Serve hot or cold with cream.

	500 watt		650 watt/2 power
a	1 minute	a	45 seconds
b	7½ minutes	b	5 minutes

	650 watt	
a	PL.7 for 45 seconds	
b	PL.8 for 5½ minutes	

Creamy Semolina

Cooking container: 4 pint casserole
Cooking time: 14 minutes
Number of servings: 4

1 pint (550 ml) milk
1 oz. (25 g) butter
1½ oz. (40 g) semolina
1 oz. (25 g) sugar

Heat the milk in a large container in the oven for [a] 5 minutes, stir in the semolina and cook for [b] 3 minutes. Add the butter and sugar, stir and return to the oven for [c] 6 minutes. To serve, sprinkle with nutmeg.

	500 watt		650 watt/2 power
a	8 minutes	a	4 minutes
b	3 minutes	b	2½ minutes
c	7 minutes	c	5-7 minutes

	650 watt	
a	PL.9 for 4 minutes	
c	PL.7 for 3 minutes	
d	PL.7 for 11-12 minutes	

Chocolate Cream Pie

Cooking container: 8" flan dish
Cooking time: 5¾ minutes
Number of servings: 5-6

8 oz. (225 g) digestive biscuit crumbs
3 oz. (75 g) butter
½ pint (275 ml) milk
1 oz. (25 g) caster sugar
1 oz. (25 g) plain flour
1½ teaspoons (7.5 ml) cornflour
2 eggs
1 oz. (25 g) butter
3 oz. (75 g) plain chocolate

Grease an 8" flan dish. Melt the butter in the oven for [a] 1 minute, stir in the biscuit crumbs and press well into the flan dish. Heat the milk and butter in the oven for [b] 2 minutes. Blend the eggs, sugar, flour and cornflour into a smooth paste and slowly add the milk to the egg mix.

Heat in the oven, stirring every 30 seconds for [c] 2 minutes. Remove from the oven and break in the chocolate. Heat for a further [d] 45 seconds. Mix well on removal from the oven. Allow to cool slightly, spoon into a biscuit case and leave in the refrigerator to set. Decorate with cream before serving.

	500 watt		650 watt/2 power
a	2½ minutes	a	45 seconds
b	3 minutes	b	2 minutes
c	3 minutes (stirring every 30 seconds)	c	1-2 minutes
d	1 minute	d	45 seconds

	650 watt	
a	PL.9 for 1 minutes	
b	PL.7 for 3 minutes	
c	PL.7 for 2½ minutes	
d	PL.7 for 1¼ minutes	

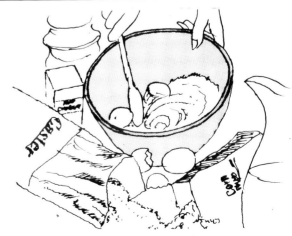

Marmalade Pudding

Container: 1½ pint bowl
Cooking time: 8 minutes
Number of servings: 4-5

5 tablespoons (75 ml) marmalade
4 oz. (100 g) flour
1 tablespoon (15 ml) baking powder
4 oz. (100 g) breadcrumbs
4 oz. (100 g) suet
1 lemon rind grated
2 oz. (50 g) brown or white sugar
2 eggs
¼ pint (150 ml) milk

Spread 1 tablespoon of marmalade over the base of a 2 pint bowl. Mix dry ingredients and lemon rind. Add remaining marmalade, eggs and milk. Mix well and place in bowl. Cover with cling film and cook for [a] 8 minutes. Stand for 2 minutes before turning out and serving.

	500 watt		650 watt/2 power
a	9 minutes (turn twice)	a	6-7 minutes
	650 watt		
a	PL.6 for 7 minutes		
	PL.9 for 2-3 minutes		

Roly-Poly Pudding

Cooking container: Cling film
Cooking time: 8 minutes
Number of servings: 5-6

8 oz. (225 g) suet crust pastry
hot jam

Roll out pastry measuring 10" x 8". Spread with warm jam leaving ½" border all round. Fold border over jam and brush with water. Roll up from one of the shorter ends and press top down sealing it. Wrap in cling film loosely. Cook for [a] 8 minutes and leave to stand for 8 minutes.

	500 watt		650 watt/2 power
a	9 minutes (turn once during cooking)	a	7 minutes
	650 watt		
a	PL.8 for 8 minutes		

Blackberry Suet Pudding

Cooking container: 1½ pint bowl
Cooking time: 8 minutes
Number of servings: 4-5

8 oz. (225 g) suet pastry
1 oz. (25 g) brown sugar
1 lb (450 g) blackberries
3 oz. (75 g) granulated sugar

Grease the bowl with butter and sprinkle with the sugar. Line with the two-thirds of the suet pastry, fill with the blackberries and sugar and cover with the remaining pastry. Cover with the clear wrap and cook in the oven for [a] 8 minutes.

	500 watt		650 watt/2 power
a	9 minutes (turn once)	a	7 minutes
	650 watt		
a	PL.7 for 10 minutes		

Brandy Coffee Cake

Cooking container: 1½ pint greased bowl
Cooking time: 4 minutes
Number of servings: 4-5

3 oz. (75 g) margarine
3 oz. (75 g) caster sugar
2 grade 2 eggs
3 oz. (75 g) self raising flour
pinch salt
¼ pint (150 ml) strong black coffee sweetened
brandy to taste

Cream sugar and margarine. Add 2 beaten eggs and mix well. Fold in flour and salt. Place mix into greased bowl. Cook for [a] 4 minutes. Leave to cool then soak with coffee/brandy mix. Turn out and decorate with cream before serving.

Suitable for freezing.

	500 watt		650 watt/2 power
a	5 minutes	a	3½ minutes
	650 watt		
a	PL.6 for 5 minutes		

Jam Sponge Pudding P.123

Steamed Syrup Pudding

Cooking container: 1½ pint basin
Cooking time: 4½ minutes
Number of servings: 4-5

4 oz. (100 g) self raising flour
2 oz. (50 g) suet
1 oz. (25 g) caster sugar
1 oz. (25 g) dark soft brown sugar
1 teaspoon (5 ml) Birds Golden Raising Agent
1 egg (grade 2)
3 fl. oz (90 ml) milk
1 level teaspoon (5 ml) vanilla essence
3 tablespoons (45 ml) syrup

Grease the basin and put the syrup in the base. Sift flour into a bowl and add the suet, sugars and raising agent. Mix ingredients with a fork. Add the milk, egg and vanilla essence and mix again with a fork. Combine milk ingredients to the dry ingredients and stir well. Spoon the mixture into the basin, cover loosely with cling film and cook for [a] 4½ minutes. Take out of the oven, remove the cling film and turn the pudding out onto a plate.

	500 watt		650 watt/2 power
a	5 minutes (turn twice)	a	7 minutes

	650 watt	
a	PL.6 for 4 minutes	
	PL.9 for 1 minute	

Rum & Pear Surprise

Cooking container: Large oval dish
Cooking time: 6 minutes
Number of servings: 4-8

4 eating pears
1½ tablespoons (25 ml) lemon juice
2½ oz. (65 g) marzipan
4 glace cherries, halved
1 oz. (25 g) butter
1 oz. (25 g) demerara sugar
2 tablespoons (30 ml) dark rum

Peel pears, cut in half and remove core. Dip in lemon juice and place in dish. Cut the marzipan into 8, put each into pear half and top with glace cherry. Combine butter, sugar and rum and heat for [a] 1 minute. Stir and spoon over pears. Cover and cook for [b] 5 minutes. Allow to stand for 5 minutes before serving.

	500 watt		650 watt/2 power
a	1-1½ minutes	a	30-45 seconds
b	6 minutes	b	4½ minutes

	650 watt	
a	PL.9 for 45 seconds	
b	PL.7 for 5 minutes	

Jam Sponge Pudding

Cooking container: 1½ pint pudding basin
Cooking time: 5½-6½ minutes   Number of servings: 4-5

4 oz. (100 g) margarine
4 oz. (100 g) caster sugar
4 oz. (100 g) plain flour
1 teaspoon (5 ml) Birds Golden Raising Agent
2 grade 2 eggs
1 tablespoon (15 ml) hot water
3 tablespoons (45 ml) jam

Cream margarine and caster sugar together until light and fluffy. Beat in the eggs and fold in the flour and raising agent. Add hot water. Place the jam into the base of the greased pudding basin and heat for [a] 30 seconds. Add the sponge mixture. Cover loosely with cling film and cook for [b] 5-6 minutes. Timing will depend on the type of jam used. Remove from oven, leave to stand for 5 minutes before turning out.

	500 watt		650 watt/2 power
a	45 seconds	a	30 seconds
b	6-7 minutes	b	5-6 minutes

	650 watt	
a	PL.9 for 30 seconds	
b	PL.9 for 5-6 minutes	

Apple Streusel Flan

Cooking container: 8½-9" pie plate or flan dish
Cooking time: pastry 4½ mins, filling 19½ mins
Number of servings: 8

Pastry

4 oz (100 g) wholemeal flour
2 oz (50 g) plain flour
3 oz (75 g) lard
2-3 tablespoons (30-45 ml) water
pinch salt

Apple filling

1½ lb (675 g) cooking apples, peeled cored and sliced
2 tablespoons (30 ml) lemon juice
3 oz (75 g) soft dark brown sugar
3 level tablespoons (45 ml) cornflour
1 level teaspoon (5 ml) cinnamon
½ teaspoon (2.5 ml) nutmeg
2 cloves (optional)

Topping

2 oz (50 g) butter
2 oz (50 g) light soft brown sugar
3 oz (75 g) flour
½ teaspoon (2.5 ml) cinnamon
1 level teaspoon (5 ml) baking powder
pinch salt

Grease 9" pie plate. Rub lard into flour until it resembles fine breadcrumbs. Add the water and form into a ball. Roll out. Cut a circle larger than dish, brush off excess flour. Put the pastry carefully into pie plate doubling under at the edge and then crimp. Prick the base. Put a piece of kitchen tissue on the pastry base and a saucer or plate to keep the pastry from bubbling up. Cook for [a] 4 minutes, remove the plate and tissue, cook for a further [b] 30 seconds. Remove from oven and prepare filling. Put lemon juice in basin, add apple and toss well. Put sugar, cornflour, cinnamon and nutmeg into a large bowl, mix well then toss the apple pieces until well coated. Place apple in pastry case and cook for [c] 4 minutes loosely covered. Topping: Put butter into a basin and cook for [d] 30 seconds until melted. Add flour, sugar, cinnamon, baking powder and salt. Mix well. Put teaspoonful of mixture over the apple, spread out lightly and cook for [e] 15 minutes.

	500 watt		650 watt/2 power
a	4 minutes	a	3 minutes
b	1 minute	b	30 seconds
c	5 minutes	c	3 minutes
d	1 minute	d	30 seconds
e	15 minutes (turn during cooking)	e	11 minutes

	650 watt	
a	PL.9 for 3 minutes	
b	PL.9 for 30 seconds	
c	PL.9 for 3 minutes	
d	PL.9 for 30 seconds	
e	PL.9 for 11 minutes	

Ice Cream Gateau

Cooking container: 2 x 6½ " 7" Cooking container
Cooking time: Approx. 2½ - 3 minutes each
Number of servings: 8-10

3 oz (75 g) butter
3 oz (75 g) caster sugar
2 grade 3 eggs, beaten
3 oz (75 g) self raising flour
1 oz (25 g) cocoa
1 level teaspoon (5 ml) baking powder
2 tablespoons (30 ml) warm water
¾ pint (375 ml) whipping cream
Orange ice cream, home made or bought

Cream butter and sugar until light and fluffy, gradually beat in the beaten eggs. Fold in sieved flour, cocoa and baking powder then add the warm water. Grease two sandwich dishes and divide the mixture between the two. Cook one at a time for [a] 2½-3 minutes. Stand for 5 minutes then turn out and allow to cool. Fill with orange ice cream. Coat all over with whipped whipping cream. Open freeze until firm, wrap in foil to store. Remove from freezer and leave in refrigerator for 1 hour before serving.

	500 watt		650 watt/2 power
a	3½-4 minutes, turn during cooking cycle.	a	2-2½ minutes

	650 watt	
a	PL.9 for 2-2½ minutes	

Orange Ice Cream

2 tins mandarin oranges, drained
½ pint (125 ml) whipping cream
1 rounded tablespoon (15 ml) sieved icing sugar
1 tablespoon (15 ml) cointreau or liqueur of your choice
Liquidise the mandarin oranges, whip up cream until quite stiff and fold in puree with the icing sugar. Put into a round container and place in freezer for 1-1¼ hours. Remove from freezer and mash with fork. Cover and return to freezer. Place in refrigerator half an hour before filling the chocolate gateau.

Eggs and Cheese

Eggs and Cheese

Microwave is the ideal cooking method for all eggs, except boiled eggs and this is one of the big **NO's** in the microwave oven. Cheese melts quickly and smoothly in the microwave oven. Remember that if cheese has been in the refrigerator and friends call unexpectedly, a minute in the microwave oven and it will be brought up to serving temperature.

As a general rule:
1 Never cook eggs in the shell
2 Always pierce the yolk of the egg with a toothpick when baking, poaching or hard cooking otherwise the pressure within the yolk as it cooks could cause it to explode.
3 With a variable power oven, cook eggs on power level 5 for better results.
4 Buttering a dish before cooking the eggs will make the dish easier to clean.

As a general rule with cheese:
1 Cheese melts best when grated and combined with milk or other liquids, use cook power or when using a variable power oven use power level 7.
2 To soften butter, cheese or ice cream, heat on power level 1 or defrost for just a few seconds until soft.
3 To melt butter, heat on cook or power level 7 until melted.
4 To clarify butter, heat on cook or power level 7 until melted and then let boil. Stand for 1 minute. The clear butter on top may then be poured off to use.

Poached Egg

Cooking container: Small dish
Cooking time: 30 seconds
Number of servings: 1

Grease a small dish, break the egg into it, prick yolk. Add a drop of melted butter and cover with kitchen paper and place in the oven. Cook for about [a] 30 seconds then allow to stand covered to finish cooking.

	500 watt		650 watt/2 power
a	50 seconds	a	30 seconds
	650 watt		
	a	PL.5 for 1¼ minutes	

Egg & Bacon Rolls

Cooking container: Serving dish
Cooking time: 5½ minutes   Number of servings: 4

4 crispy bread rolls
2 rashers bacon, finely chopped
2 oz. (50 g) mushrooms, finely chopped
4 eggs
salt and pepper

Slice off the top of the bread roll and scoop out the centre bread. Place the mushrooms and bacon into the microwave oven and cook uncovered for [a] 3 minutes. Drain off excess liquid and share this mix between each of the bread rolls. On top of the bacon break an egg into each roll, sprinkle with salt and pepper, cover with the top of the bread roll and place into oven. Cook for [b] 2½-3 minutes. Remember to prick the yolks before placing the eggs into the oven. Stand for 1 minute before serving.

	500 watt		650 watt/2 power
a	4 minutes	a	2½-3 minutes
b	4½-5 minutes	b	2½-3 minutes
	650 watt		
	a	PL.7 for 3 minutes	
	a	PL.7 for 4 minutes	

Pricking egg yolk

126

Cheese & Onion Bake

Cooking container: 3 pint casserole
Cooking time: 25-30 minutes   Number of servings: 4

1¼ lb (575 g) peeled potatoes
1 oz (25 g) butter
1 large onion, finely sliced
½ pint (275 ml) milk
salt and pepper
5 oz (125 g) grated cheese

Put the potatoes into the casserole add 6 tablespoons of water. Cook covered for [a] 6 minutes, leave to stand covered. Melt the butter in a basin add the sliced onion, cook for [b] 4 minutes until transparent. Drain and slice the potatoes, lightly grease the casserole dish and place the potatoes, onion and cheese in alternate layers. Season the milk and pour over the cheese mixture. Cover and cook for [c] 15-20 minutes, until the potato is cooked. Leave to stand for 5 minutes, sprinkle with crushed cornflakes.

	500 watt		650 watt/2 power
a	6 minutes	a	5 minutes
b	4½ minutes	b	3 minutes
c	20 minutes	c	15 minutes

	650 watt	
a	PL.9 for 5 minutes	
b	PL.9 for 3 minutes	
c	PL.7 for 20 minutes	

Eggs baked in Cream

Cooking container: Individual cocotte dishes or muffin pan
Cooking time: 5½ minutes
Number of servings: 4

½oz. (15 g) butter
1 fl. oz. (30 ml) cream
4 eggs size 2
salt
pepper

Grease each of the containers, place in 1 teaspoon of cream. Break the egg into dish, prick with skewer, cover with 1 teaspoon of cream and sprinkle with salt and pepper. Cook 4 eggs for [a] 5½ minutes on defrost. Stand for 2 minutes before serving.

	500 watt		650 watt/2 power
a	7½ minutes on defrost (turn around halfway through cooking time).	a	5 minutes on defrost

	650 watt	
a	PL.5 for 4-4½ minutes	

Cheese Shrimp Bake

Cooking container: Round shallow dish
Cooking time: 30-32 minutes
Number of servings: 4-5

8 slices white bread
1 large can of shrimps, drained and rinsed
2 sticks of celery, finely chopped
1 medium onion, finely chopped
1 small can condensed mushroom soup
dash of Worcestershire sauce
4 oz. (100 g) cheddar cheese, grated
6 fl. oz. (180 ml) milk
3 eggs, beaten
2 oz. (50 g) butter)

Place four slices of the bread in the base of a large shallow dish. Cover with the shrimps, onion and celery. Mix the soup with the sauce and pour over the shrimp mix. Sprinkle on the cheese and cover with the remaining bread. Beat together the eggs and the milk, pour over the bread and dot with the butter. Cover and set in the refrigerator for 30 minutes. Cook in the oven for [a] 30-32 minutes on defrost. Place under the grill if a crisp finish is required.

	500 watt		650 watt/2 power
a	20-23 minutes (turn once)	a	28-30 minutes on defrost

	650 watt	
a	PL.4 for 32 minutes	

Eggs Florentine

Cooking container: Flat dish
Cooking time: Approx. 14½-16½ minutes
Number of servings: 4
4 eggs
1 lb (450 g) cooked spinach
salt
pepper
1 oz. (25 g) butter
¾ oz. (20 g) cornflour
½ pint (275 ml) milk
3 oz. (75 g) grated cheese

Place the cooked spinach into a flat dish making 4 wells in each corner. Break the eggs into these wells. In a 2 pint bowl place the cornflour, butter and milk. Season lightly with salt and pepper. Heat in the microwave oven for [a] 3½ minutes stirring well every minute. Add in the grated cheese and heat for a further [b] minute. Stand to one side. Place the spinach and eggs into the microwave oven and heat for approximately [c] 8-10 minutes or until eggs are almost set. Remove from oven and heat the cheese sauce for [d] 2 minutes. Pour the sauce over the eggs and serve. This can be browned under the grill if desired.

	500 watt		650 watt/2 power
a	4 minutes	a	3 minutes
b	1½ minutes	b	1 minute
c	11-12 minutes	c	6-8 minutes
d	1½ minutes	d	1½ minutes
650 watt			
a	PL.9 for 3 minutes		
b	PL.9 for 1 minute		
c	PL.7 for 8-10 minutes		
d	PL.9 for 1½ minutes		

Fried Eggs

Cooking container: Browning dish
Cooking time: 1½ minutes
Number of servings: 4
4 eggs size 2
½ oz. (15 g) margarine

Heat browning dish for [a] 4 minutes then melt in margarine.Break in eggs. Prick yolks and cover with lid and cook for [b] 1½ minutes. Stand for 1 minute before serving.

	500 watt		650 watt/2 power
a	5 minutes	a	4 minutes
b	2½ minutes	b	1-1¼ minutes
650 watt			
a	PL.9 for 3½ minutes		
b	PL.7 for 1¼ minutes		

Fondue

Cooking container: 2 pint casserole
Cooking time: 9 minutes
Number of servings: 4-5

¼ pint (150 ml) dry white wine
¼ pint (150 ml) milk
4 oz. (100 g) gruyere cheese
4 oz. (100 g) emmental cheese
1 tablespoon (15 ml) flour
1 liquor glass kirsch
Little pepper
1 clove garlic crushed

Rub the inside of a 2 pint casserole with garlic. Place the wine and milk into the casserole and heat for [a] 2 minutes. Add the cheese and flour. Stir well and heat for [b] 4 minutes. Add the seasoning and kirsch and heat for a further [c] 3 minutes or until mixture is thick and creamy.

	500 watt		650 watt/2 power
a	3 minutes	a	1½ minutes
b	5½ minutes	b	3½ minutes
c	4-5 minutes	c	2-3 minutes
650 watt			
a	PL.7 for 2 minutes		
b	PL.7 for 4 minutes		
c	PL.7 for 3-5 minutes		

Welsh Rarebit P.129

Scrambled Eggs

Cooking container: Pyrex jug 2 pint
Cooking time: 3 minutes
Number of servings: 2

4 eggs
2 tablespoons (30 ml) milk
½ oz. (15 g) butter
salt and pepper

Beat together all the ingredients in a glass container.
Heat in the oven for [a] 2 minutes. Stir to break up the
setting egg and return to the oven for [b] 1 minute. Stir
and serve. If you require a drier egg, return the mix to the
oven for a few seconds.

	500 watt		650 watt/2 power
a	2 minutes	a	2 minutes
b	2 minutes	b	1¾ minutes
	650 watt		
a	PL.9 for 2 minutes		
b	PL.9 for 1¾ minutes		

Spanish Omelette

Cooking container: Large pie plate
Cooking time: 15 minutes
Number of servings: 2-3

5 eggs
salt and pepper
2 cooked potatoes, sliced
¼ red pepper, sliced finely
4 mushrooms, sliced
1 onion finely chopped
1 oz. (25 g) butter

Sauté onion, peppers and butter in dish for [a] 4 minutes.
Add potatoes and mushrooms and cook for [b] 3
minutes. Beat eggs together lightly with salt and pepper.
Pour over vegetables and cook on defrost for [c] 8
minutes or until set. Stir gently moving outer edges to
middle. Place under the grill before serving.

	500 watt		650 watt/2 power
a	4 minutes	a	4 minutes
b	4 minutes	b	3 minutes
c	2½ minutes	c	7 minutes
	Approx.		
	8 minutes		
	on defrost		
	650 watt		
a	PL.9 for 4 minutes		
b	PL.9 for 3 minutes		
c	PL.5 for 6 minutes		

Quiche Lorraine

Cooking container: Serving plate
Cooking time: 7½ minutes
Number of servings: 4

1 x 7-7½" flan case pre-baked
4 oz. (90 g) chopped bacon
2 grade 3 eggs
3 oz. (75 g) cheese
¼ pint (150 ml) milk
1 teaspoon (5 ml) mustard
salt and pepper

Place the flan case onto the serving plate and spread the base with the mustard. Place the chopped bacon onto a piece of kitchen paper, cook in the microwave oven for [a] 2 minutes. Sprinkle the chopped bacon over the base of the flan case. Cut the cheese into thin finger strips and arrange in a spoke pattern over the bacon. Gently beat the eggs with the milk and season. Pour over the bacon and cheese and place the flan into the microwave oven. Cook on full power for [b] 2½ minutes then turn to defrost and cook for another [c] 4 minutes. Leave to stand for 10 minutes before cutting. Serve hot or cold.

	500 watt		650 watt/2 power
a	3 minutes	a	2 minutes
b	4 minutes	b	3 minutes
c	6-8 minutes on defrost	c	3½-4 minutes

650 watt	
a	PL.9 for 2 minutes
b	PL.9 for 3 minutes
c	PL.7 for 5 minutes

Macaroni Cheese

Cooking container: 2 pint casserole
Cooking time: 29½ minutes
Number of servings: 4

2 pints (1.15 litres) hot water
8 oz. (225 g) macaroni
2 teaspoons (10 ml) oil
salt
¾ oz. (20 g) butter
¾ oz. (20 g) flour
good pinch dry mustard
1 teaspoon (5 ml) paprika pepper
¾ pint (425 ml) milk
6 oz. (175 g) grated cheese
4 oz. (100 g) bacon

Cook bacon on absorbent paper for [a] 4 minutes (until crisp) and leave to cool. In 2 pint casserole place hot water, macaroni, salt and oil. Cook for [b] 15 minutes covered then leave to stand. Melt butter for [c] 1 minute in small casserole. Add flour, stir and cook for [d] 30 seconds. Add mustard and paprika pepper — gradually stir in milk. Return to oven for [e] 4 minutes. Stir well after 2 minutes and on removal from oven. Drain macaroni and pour sauce over. Stir in cheese and heat for [f] 2 minutes. Crumble bacon over cheese, heat for [g] 3 minutes and serve.

	500 watt		650 watt/2 power
a	5 minutes	a	1 minute
b	15 minutes	b	15 minutes
c	1 minute	c	30 seconds
d	1 minute	d	30 seconds
e	5 minutes	e	5 minutes
f	3 minutes	f	2 minutes
g	4 minutes	g	3 minutes

650 watt	
a	PL.9 for 3 minutes
b	PL.9 for 17 minutes
c	PL.9 for 1 minutes
d	PL.7 for 1 minute
e	PL.9 for 5 minutes
f	PL.8 for 2 minutes
g	PL.8 for 3 minutes

Welsh Rarebit

See colour plate page 129

Cooking container: 2 pint bowl
Cooking time: 5 minutes
Number of servings: 4-6

8 oz. (225 g) cheese (a mixture of Leicester and Stilton)
1 tablespoon (15 ml) made-up mustard
salt
pepper
4 tablespoons (60 ml) brown ale

Place all the ingredients into a 2 pint bowl. Heat for approximately [a] 5 minutes or until mixture is bubbling. Stir every 2 minutes. Pour over slices of toast. This can be placed under the grill before serving.

500 watt		650 watt/2 power	
a	6 minutes	a	4 minutes
650 watt			
a	PL.7 for 5 minutes approx.		

Sweet Omelette

Cooking container: Browning dish
Cooking time: 2½-3 minutes
Number of servings: 1

2 eggs separated
1 teaspoon (5 ml) ground almonds
1 teaspoon (5 ml) caster sugar
1 tablespoon (15 ml) cold water
½ oz. (15 g) butter

Heat browning dish in microwave oven for [a] 4 minutes. Whisk the egg whites until stiff. Whisk gently the egg yolks with the water, sugar and almonds. Melt the butter in browning dish. Fold egg yolks into egg white and place into browning dish — cook for [b] 2½-3 minutes then spread with a little jam and fold in half.

500 watt		650 watt/2 power	
a	5 minutes	a	3 minutes
b	3½-4 minutes (turn halfway through cooking).	b	2-2½ minutes
650 watt			
a	PL.8 for 3½ minutes		
b	PL.7 for 2-2½ minutes		

Creme Caramel

Cooking container: 7"-7½" deep round dish
Cooking time: 34 minutes
Number of servings: 6

5 oz. (125 g) sugar
¼ pint (150 ml) water
1 pint (550 ml) milk
4 large eggs
vanilla essence

Into cake dish place water and 4 oz. sugar. Heat for [a] 3 minutes and stir. Heat for a further [b] 11-15 minutes (until syrup turns golden brown) and add 2 tablespoons hot water. Heat milk for [c] 3 minutes. Whisk eggs with 1 oz. sugar and vanilla essence. Whisk in milk. Strain milk into dish and cook on defrost for [d] 20 minutes (until set). Stand for 10 minutes before serving.

500 watt		650 watt/2 power	
a	4 minutes	a	3 minutes
b	17-18 minutes	b	11 minutes
c	4 minutes	c	2½ minutes
d	20-22 minutes (turn once)	d	20 minutes on defrost
650 watt			
a	PL.7 for 4 minutes		
b	PL.9 for 11-14 minutes		
c	PL.9 for 4 minutes		
d	PL.4 for 12-15 minutes		

Rice Pasta Cereals and Pulses

Rice Pasta Cereals and Pulses

These can all be easily cooked in the microwave oven. To save time boil the required amount of water in a kettle. The time cooking in the oven will be just a little less than with conventional cooking but of course the kitchen is not filled with steam and your container is always easier to clean.

As a general rule:
1 Cook most items on full power or power level 9, except for milk-based puddings such as rice puddings which should be cooked on defrost or power level 3.
2 Cook covered in a large glass or ceramic dish.
3 Bring water to the boil before adding pasta.

Microwave Method

Pasta. When cooking long pasta such as lasagne or spaghetti, lay it into an oblong dish, cover with the required amount of boiling water adding a teaspoon of salt and a tablespoon of oil. Halfway through the cooking time gently distribute the pasta and cover. Allow to stand for 5 minutes before draining.

Rice. When cooking rice, this can be cooked either in salted water or in a flavoured stock. Allow to stand for 5 minutes before serving the rice.

Pulses. When cooking pulses in the microwave oven the cooking time again is approximately the same as when done conventionally.

Spaghetti, preparation for cooking

134

Pasta and Rice Cooking Chart

Brown Rice *8 oz. (raw)* *1 lb. 6 oz. (cooked)*	Cook in 2 pints boiling salt water for 30 minutes. Stand for 3-4 minutes.
Egg Noodles . *8 oz. (raw)* *1 lb. 6 oz. (cooked)*	Cook in 2 pints boiling salt water for 7-8 minutes. Stand for 2 minutes.
Spaghetti *8 oz. (raw)* *1 lb. 6 oz. (cooked)*	Add 1 dessertspoon of oil to 2 pints boiling salt water and cook for 13 minutes. Stand for 2 minutes.
Pasta Shells *8 oz. (raw)* *1 lb. 6 oz. (cooked)*	Add 1 dessertspoon of oil to 3 pints boiling salt water and cook for 16 minutes. Stand for 2 minutes.
Macaroni *8 oz. (raw)* *1 lb. 6 oz. (cooked)*	Add 1 dessertspoon of oil to 2 pints boiling salt water and cook for 16 minutes. Stand for 2 minutes.
Long Grain Rice *8 oz. (raw)* *1 lb. 6 oz. (cooked)*	Cook in 2 pints boiling salt water for 9-10 minutes. Stand for 5 minutes.
Lasagne *8 oz. (raw)*	Cook in 2 pints of boiling salt water for 16 minutes. Stand for 2 minutes.
Savoury Rice *4 oz. (raw)* *14 oz. (cooked)*	Cook in ¾ pint boiling water for 18 minutes. Stand for 3 minutes.
Parboiled long grain rice ★ *8 oz. (raw)* *1 lb. 6 oz. (cooked)*	Place in dish with 2 pints boiling water and 1 teaspoon salt and cook for 16 minutes. Stand for 3 minutes.
Heat and serve Rice *9 oz.*	Heat 4 fl. oz. water and salt for 2 minutes, add rice and cook for 3 minutes. Stand for 2 minutes.

Note: Once the water is boiling, timings are approximate regardless of wattage.

★ e.g. Uncle Ben's

Porridge

Cooking container: 3 pint dish
Cooking time: 10 minutes
Number of servings: 2-3

1 cup porridge oats
1 cup milk
2 cups water
good pinch of salt

Mix all the ingredients together and place in the oven for [a] 10 minutes. Stir twice during this cycle. For a quicker result use hot water.

500 watt		650 watt/2 power	
a	13 minutes	a	9 minutes
650 watt			
a	PL.9 for 9 minutes		

Lentils with Mushrooms

Cooking container: 3 pint casserole
Cooking time: 73 minutes
Number of servings: 4-5

8 oz. (225 g) continental lentils (with husks on)
½ pint (275 ml) chicken stock
14 oz. (397 g) can tomatoes
1 tablespoon (15 ml) oil
2 teaspoons (10 ml) basil
salt
8 oz. (225 g) sliced mushrooms
3 stalks celery chopped
2 onions

Heat lentils in 1½ pints water in the oven for [a] 8 minutes. Stand for 4 hours. Sauté celery and onions with oil in casserole dish for [b] 3 minutes. Add mushrooms, cover and cook for [c] 2 minutes. Add all other ingredients and cook for [d] 60 minutes on defrost.

500 watt		650 watt/2 power	
a	10 minutes	a	8 minutes
b	4 minutes	b	2½ minutes
c	3 minutes	c	2 minutes
d	80 minutes defrost	d	60 minutes
650 watt			
a	PL.9 for 8 minutes		
b	PL.7 for 3 minutes		
c	PL.7 for 2 minutes		
d	PL.4 for 60 minutes		

Lasagne

Cooking container: 2½ pint casserole
Cooking time: 46 minutes
Number of servings: 4-5

8 strips lasagne
½ teaspoon (2.5 ml) oil
2 pints (1150 ml) boiling water
1 lb (450 g) minced beef
1 large chopped onion
14 oz. (397 g) can tomatoes
1 beef stock cube
good pinch marjoram
2 tablespoons (30 ml) tomato purée
salt and pepper

Cheese Sauce
1 packet Cheese Sauce Mix
½ pint (300 ml) milk

Place boiling water and oil in large container. Cook lasagne for [a] 16 minutes. Leave to stand for 5 minutes before draining. Place mince and onion into a 2½ pint casserole and cook for [b] 5 minutes. Add all the other ingredients and cook uncovered for [c] 12 minutes. Make up cheese sauce as directed. Cook in oven for [d] 3 minutes. Place lasagne and mincemeat mixture in layers in a suitable dish, finishing with lasagne. Top with cheese sauce and return to oven for [e] 10 minutes.

500 watt		650 watt/2 power	
a	16 minutes	a	16 minutes
b	6 minutes	b	5 minutes
c	15 minutes	c	11 minutes
d	4 minutes	d	2½-3 minutes
e	12 minutes	e	10 minutes
650 watt			
a	PL.9 for 16 minutes		
b	PL.7 for 6 minutes		
c	PL.7 for 13 minutes		
d	PL.9 for 2½-3 minutes		
e	PL.8 for 10 minutes		

Almond Sesame Noodles

Cooking container: 2½ pint casserole
Cooking time: 16 minutes
Number of servings: 4

8 oz. (225 g) noodles cooked
2 oz. (50 g) butter
2 oz. (50 g) toasted flaked almonds
2 tablespoons (30 ml) toasted sesame seeds

Toast almonds by spreading them onto a glass dish and heating for [a] 7-8 minutes until brown (shake frequently). Brown sesame seeds by the same method for [b] 4-5 minutes. Melt butter and stir in seeds and almonds. Add noodles, heat for [c] 3 minutes and toss before serving.

	500 watt		650 watt/2 power
a	8-9 minutes	a	6½-7 minutes
b	5-6 minutes	b	3-4 minutes
c	5 minutes	c	2½ minutes
	650 watt		
	a	PL.8 for 7-8 minutes	
	b	PL.8 for 4-5 minutes	
	c	PL.8 for 3 minutes	

Rice Pudding

Cooking container: 2½ pint dish
Cooking time: 65 minutes
Number of servings: 4

1 pint (550 ml) milk
1 oz (25 g) butter
1 oz (25 g) sugar
2 oz (50 g) short grain rice
nutmeg

Heat the milk in the dish for [a] 5 minutes. Stir in butter, sugar and rice. Cook uncovered for [b] 50 minutes on defrost, then [c] 10 minutes on full power. Stand for 5 minutes before serving and sprinkle with nutmeg.

	500 watt		650 watt/2 power
a	6 minutes	a	4 minutes
b	60 minutes defrost	b	60 minutes defrost
c	5 minutes full power	c	5 minutes full power
	650 watt		
	a	PL.9 for 4 minutes	
	b	PL.3 for 50 minutes	
	c	PL.4 for 13 minutes	

Pease Pudding

Cooking container: 4 pint casserole
Cooking time: 71 minutes
Number of servings: 4-6

8 oz. (225 g) split dried peas
1 oz. (25 g) butter
1 egg
salt and pepper
bacon scraps
chopped parsley
1 teaspoon (5 ml) salt

In a covered casserole heat peas and water (water to cover peas by 2") for [a] 8 minutes. Stand covered for 4 hours. Drain peas and cover with fresh water, add bacon scraps and cook covered for [b] 60 minutes or until peas are soft (note: Liquid will need topping up after 35 minutes). Peas need to be kept very moist. Drain liquid from peas and pass through sieve or blend in liquidizer or food processor. Add butter, egg, parsley, salt and pepper. If very thick, add 2 tablespoons of liquid. Turn into 2 pint bowl. Heat covered for [c] 3 minutes when required. Turn out onto serving plate.

	500 watt		650 watt/2 power
a	9 minutes	a	7 minutes
b	65 minutes	b	55 minutes
c	3½ minutes	c	2½ minutes
	650 watt		
	a	PL.9 for 7 minutes	
	b	PL.9 for 55 minutes	
	c	PL.8 for 3 minutes	

Risotto

Cooking container: 4 pint casserole
Cooking time: 26 minutes
Number of servings: 3-4

2 chicken stock cubes
8 oz. (225 g) long grain quick cook rice
1 red pepper, chopped
1 onion, chopped
4 oz. (100 g) peas, frozen
½ oz. (15 g) butter
8 oz. (225 g) chicken, sliced
8 oz. (225 g) prawns
1½ pints (750 ml) hot water
salt and pepper
1 teaspoon (5 ml) parsley

Place onions, pepper and butter into casserole and heat for [a] 4 minutes. Add rice, stock cubes and hot water. Cook for [b] 10 minutes uncovered. Add all other ingredients, cover and cook for a further [c] 12 minutes. Stand for 5 minutes before serving.

Suitable for freezing.

	500 watt		650 watt/2 power	
a	4 minutes	a	4 minutes
b	15 minutes	b	9 minutes
c	15 minutes	c	10 minutes
650 watt				
a	PL.9 for 4 minutes			
b	PL.9 for 9 minutes			
c	PL.9 for 10 minutes			

Paella

See colour plate page 139

Cooking container: 4 pint casserole
Cooking time: 30 minutes
Number of servings: 4

4 oz. (100 g) long grain rice
4 chicken drum sticks
4 oz. (100 g) prawns
1 tablespoon (15 ml) olive oil
1 clove garlic, chopped
½ red pepper, chopped
6 oz. (175 g) frozen peas
1 pint (550 ml) chicken stock
1 onion, chopped
8 mussels
saffron

Brown chicken portions in frying pan. Sauté onion, garlic, pepper and rice with oil in a 4 pint casserole for [a] 5 minutes. Stir in stock, saffron and chicken. Cook covered for [b] 15 minutes. Add all other ingredients and heat for [c] 10 minutes. Stand for 5 minutes before serving.

Suitable for freezing.

	500 watt		650 watt/2 power	
a	7 minutes	a	4 minutes
b	18 minutes	b	12 minutes
c	15 minutes	c	10 minutes
650 watt				
a	PL.9 for 4 minutes			
b	PL.9 for 12 minutes			
c	PL.9 for 10 minutes			

Paella P.139

Mediterranean Rice

Cooking container: 3-4 pint casserole
Cooking time: 22 minutes
Number of servings: 4
12 oz. (350 g) cooked, chopped chicken
8 oz. (225 g) long grain rice, cooked
8 oz. (225 g) shelled prawns
1 x 7¾ oz. tuna fish
1 green pepper, chopped
½ lb (225 g) sliced tomatoes
1 small can sweet corn
¼ lb (100 g) sliced mushrooms
1 chopped onion
1 small tin pineapple pieces
Cook onion and pepper for [a] 3 minutes. Add mushrooms, cook for [b] 2 minutes. Add the sweet corn, pineapple, tuna fish, chicken and rice and cook for [c] 5 minutes. Mix in prawns and tomatoes. Season, cover and heat until piping hot for [d] 12 minutes. Stand for 5 mins.

	500 watt		650 watt/2 power
a	3½ minutes	a	3 minutes
b	2 minutes	b	1½ minutes
c	6 minutes	c	4 minutes
d	14 minutes	d	12 minutes

	650 watt	
a	PL.7 for 3 minutes
b	PL.7 for 2 minutes
c	PL.9 for 4 minutes
d	PL.9 for 12 minutes

Fried Rice

Cooking container: Browning skillet
Cooking time: 5 minutes
Number of servings: 3-4
8 oz. (225 g) cooked long grain rice (well drained)
2 teaspoons (10 ml) oil
salt and pepper
2 finely chopped spring onions   1 beaten egg
Heat the browning dish for [a] 5 minutes. Add oil and stir in rice. Heat for [b] 2 minutes. Stir in onions and seasoning and heat for a further [c] 2 minutes. Make a hollow in the centre of the rice. Gently stir in the beaten egg and cook for [d] 1 minute.

	500 watt		650 watt/2 power
a	6 minutes	a	6 minutes
b	3 minutes	b	2 minutes
c	3 minutes	c	2 minutes
d	2 minutes	d	45 seconds

	650 watt	
a	PL.8 for 5 minutes
b	PL.8 for 2 minutes
c	PL.8 for 2 minutes
d	PL.8 for 1 minute

Pasta with Chicken Livers

Cooking container: 2½ pint casserole/4 pint casserole
Cooking time: 55 minutes
Number of servings: 4
8 oz. (225 g) chopped chicken livers
3 onions chopped
¾ pint (425 ml) chicken stock
6 oz. (175 g) skinned tomatoes
2 tablespoons (30 ml) tomato purée
4 oz. (100 g) chopped mushrooms
1 teaspoon (5 ml) chopped parsley
6 oz. (175 g) Tagliatelle
Cook the Tagliatelle in 3 pints of boiling water for [a] 12 minutes with salt and 1 dessertspoon of oil. Stand for 5 minutes, drain and place into serving dish. In a 2½ pint casserole place onion, liver and tomatoes and cook for [b] 10 minutes. Add all other ingredients and cook for [c] 30 minutes uncovered. Pour sauce over Tagliatelle. Sprinkle with 2 oz. Mazzarella cheese. Heat for [d] 3 minutes.

	500 watt		650 watt/2 power
a	13 minutes	a	10 minutes
b	13 minutes	b	8 minutes
c	35 minutes	c	25 minutes
d	4 minutes	d	2½ minutes

	650 watt	
a	PL.9 for 10 minutes
b	PL.7 for 10 minutes
c	PL.9 for 25 minutes
d	PL.8 for 3 minutes

Fried rice

Spaghetti con Funghi

Cooking container: 4 pint casserole/2½ pint casserole
Cooking time: 43 minutes
Number of servings: 4

2 rashers chopped bacon
12 oz. (350 g) skinned tomatoes
12 oz. (350 g) button mushrooms
1 teaspoon (5 ml) dried oregano
1 bay leaf
¼ pint (150 ml) red wine
¼ pint (150 ml) beef stock
salt and pepper
8 oz. (225 g) spaghetti

Cook spaghetti for [a] 10 minutes in 3 pints of boiling water. Stand for 5 minutes, drain and place into serving dish. Into casserole place chopped tomatoes and bacon and cook covered for [b] 5 minutes. Stir, add all other ingredients and cook uncovered for [c] 25 minutes. Pour over spaghetti. Heat in the oven for [d] 3 minutes then sprinkle with parmesan cheese before serving.

	500 watt		650 watt/2 power
a	12 minutes	a	10 minutes
b	7 minutes	b	4½ minutes
c	28 minutes	c	20 minutes
d	4 minutes	d	2½ minutes
	650 watt		
a	PL.9 for 10 minutes		
b	PL.7 for 5 minutes		
c	PL.9 for 20 minutes		
d	PL.8 for 2½ minutes		

Brown Rice Salad

Cooking container: 4 pint casserole
Cooking time: 33 minutes
Number of servings: 4-6

6 oz. (175 g) long grain rice (brown)
¼ diced cucumber
4 sliced spring onions
¼ green pepper chopped
¼ red pepper chopped
2 oz. (50 g) green olives
2 tablespoons (30 ml) oil
1 tablespoon (15 ml) lemon juice
1 teaspoon (5 ml) chopped parsley
good pinch garlic salt
salt and pepper
1 lb (450 g) cooked meat or fish

Place rice into 4 pint bowl, cover with 1½ pints of cold water and cook for [a] 33 minutes. Rinse in cold water and when cooked add to vegetables and meat or fish. Combine the oil, lemon, parsley, garlic salt and pepper. Keep the dressing in a separate container and mix into salad just before serving.

	500 watt		650 watt/2 power
a	40-45 minutes	a	30 minutes
	650 watt		
	a	PL.9 for 30 minutes	

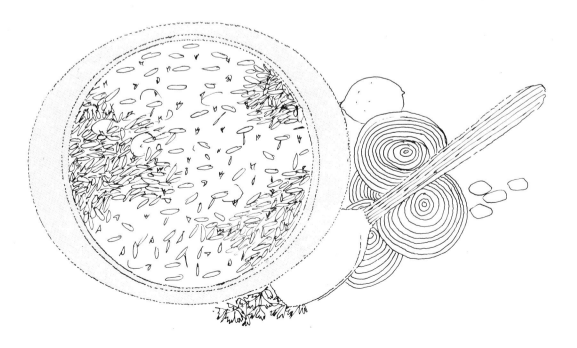

Chicken & Tuna Ring

Cooking container: 3-4 pint casserole
Cooking time: 21 minutes
Number of servings: 4

1 tablespoon (15 ml) oil
1 large onion
8 oz. (225 g) long grain rice
1 pint (550 ml) chicken stock
¼ oz. (7 g) butter
8 oz. (225 g) chopped cooked chicken
1 small tin mushrooms (drained)
1 tablespoon (15 ml) lemon juice
1 can (295 g) condensed chicken soup
2 tablespoons (30 ml) milk
7 oz. can tuna fish, flaked
Tabasco sauce
freshly milled pepper and salt

Soften chopped onion in oil for [a] 2 minutes in 4 pint
casserole. Add rice and stock, cover and cook for [b] 12
minutes or until rice absorbs stock and becomes light and
fluffy. If any excess liquid remains, drain and leave rice
dry. Press well down into ring mould and cover. Leave to
one side until required. Mix butter, mushrooms and
lemon juice together. Cook for [c] 1 minute, stir and then
cook for a further [d] minute. Add soup, milk, flaked
fish, chicken, salt and pepper. Cook for [e] 2½ minutes,
stir, cook for further [f] 2½ minutes. Add Tabasco and
seasoning to taste. Turn out ring onto serving plate. Pour
sauce into centre and over edge of ring.

	500 watt		650 watt/2 power
a	3 minutes	a	2 minutes
b	15-18 minutes	b	11 minutes
c	1 minute	c	30 seconds
d	1 minute	d	1 minute
e	3 minutes	e	2 minutes
f	2 minutes	f	2 minutes

	650 watt
a	PL.7 for 2 minutes
b	PL.9 for 11 minutes
c	PL.7 for 1 minute
d	PL.7 for 1 minute
e	PL.9 for 2 minutes
f	PL.9 for 2 minutes

Spaghetti Bolognese

Cooking container: 3 pint casserole
Cooking time: 24 minutes
Number of servings: 2-4

1 chopped green pepper
1 crushed clove of garlic
½ glass red wine
1 lb (450 g) minced beef
¼ lb (100 g) mushrooms, sliced
small tin tomatoes
2 tablespoons (30 ml) tomato purée
fresh or dried oregano
1 bay leaf
1 oz. (25 g) butter
2 tablespoons (30 ml) mango sauce
1 onion chopped
seasoning

Melt butter in 3 pint casserole. Add chopped onion,
garlic and pepper, cook for [a] 3 minutes. Add
mushrooms and cook for a further [b] 2 minutes. Stir in
beef and cook covered for [c] 6 minutes. Stir halfway
through. Add tomatoes, puree, red wine, oregano,
mango sauce, bay leaf and seasoning. Bring back to
simmer for [d] 10 minutes. Cover and cook on defrost
for [e] 16 minutes.
Serve with spaghetti sprinkled with Parmesan cheese.
(See introduction to this section for cooking spaghetti).
Suitable for freezing.

	500 watt		650 watt/2 power
a	4 minutes	a	3 minutes
b	3 minutes	b	1½ minutes
c	10 minutes	c	5 minutes
d	15 minutes	d	10 minutes
e	30 minutes on defrost	e	15 minutes on defrost

	650 watt
a	PL.9 for 3 minutes
b	PL.9 for 1½ minutes
c	PL.9 for 5 minutes
d	PL.9 for 10 minutes
e	PL.3 for 20 minutes

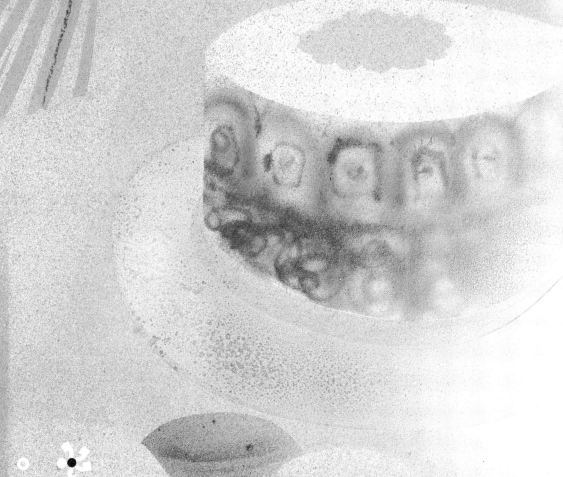

Cakes and Biscuits

Cakes and Biscuits

Cakes and biscuits, whether your own favourite recipe or from a packet mix, can be cooked quickly in the microwave oven but in some cases the texture is different from cakes cooked in a conventional oven.

As a general rule:

1 Use a round dish, ring mould or narrow oblong shaped dish
2 Do not flour cooking container; either line base and sides with greased greaseproof paper or grease and sprinkle lightly with caster sugar.
3 Remove cake from oven before completely dry on surface.
4 Test for doneness with a toothpick which should come out of the cake cleanly and edges of cake should be coming away from sides.
5 On removal from the oven stand cake for 5 minutes before turning out onto greaseproof paper.
6 Use 2 layers of paper cases when cooking fairy cakes.
7 For packet mixes and own recipes, add approximately 25% extra liquid when mixing cake.
8 Use deep dishes in the oven to avoid mix overflowing.
9 Avoid over creaming and mixing cake mixtures, especially when using a food processor.

Microwave method:

1 Prepare cake mix.
2 Place into dish which has been lightly greased and lined at base.
3 Even out surface.
4 Cook in oven until just coming away from sides.
5 Allow cake to cool in dish for 5 minutes before turning out.

Chocolate Shortbread

Cooking container: Shallow dish
Cooking time: 13 minutes
Number of servings: 12-16

4 oz. (100 g) butter
3 oz. (75 g) soft brown sugar
7 oz. (175 g) flour

Icing:

6 oz. (150 g) plain cooking chocolate

Topping:

3 tablespoons (45 ml) sweetened condensed milk
1 tablespoon (15 ml) golden syrup
4 oz. (100 g) butter
2 oz. (50 g) soft brown sugar

Cream butter and sugar together, add the flour and mix well. Press into a shallow dish and prick the surface. Cook for [a] 4 minutes. Put all the topping ingredients into a basin and cook for [b] 2 minutes. Stir well after 1 minute. Pour the topping onto the shortbread and cook for [c] 4½-5 minutes until bubbling. After 3 minutes give the dish a little shake to even out topping. Remove from the oven and leave to cool. Break the chocolate into squares and put into a basin. Cook for [d] 2½ minutes until smooth then pour onto cooled shortbread.

	500 watt			650 watt/2 power
a	4½ minutes		a	4 minutes
b	2½ minutes		b	2 minutes
c	5 minutes		c	4-4½ minutes
d	3 minutes		d	2-2½ minutes

	650 watt
a	PL.9 for 4 minutes
b	PL.9 for 2 minutes
c	PL.9 for 4-4½ minutes
d	PL.9 for 2-2½ minutes

Battenburg Cake

Cooking container: 2 greased loaf shaped containers
Cooking time: 4½ minutes
Number of servings: 6-8

2 standard eggs
4 oz. (100 g) caster sugar
4 oz. (100 g) soft margarine
5 oz. (150 g) self raising flour
10 oz. (300 g) marzipan
red colouring
strawberry flavouring
almond flavouring
jam
water

Cream margarine and sugar, add beaten eggs, fold in flour and add enough water to make a soft dropping consistency. Divide the mixture into two. Add a few drops of red colouring and strawberry flavouring to one half, and a few drops of almond essence to the other. Put into two greased microwave loaf shaped containers and leave to rest for 5 minutes. Place in microwave oven and cook for [a] 4½ minutes. Leave to stand until cool and turn out. Spread jam over one sponge and place other on top. Cut through both vertically. Spread jam on cut halves and reverse one side to make a chequered section. Roll out marzipan thinly into a rectangle large enough to enclose the cake. Wrap the marzipan around the cake with join at the bottom. Dust with a little caster sugar.

	500 watt		650 watt/2 power
a	8-9 minutes	a	3½-4 minutes
	650 watt		
	a	PL.9 for 3½-4 minutes	

Chocolate Cake

Cooking container: 7"-7½" round deep dish
Cooking time: 4½-5 minutes
Number of servings: 6-8
4 oz. (100 g) margarine
3 oz. (75 g) self raising flour
4 oz. (100 g) caster sugar
1 oz. (25 g) drinking chocolate
2 tablespoons (30 ml) water
2 grade 3 eggs, beaten
½ teaspoon (2.5 ml) baking powder

Into a large mixing bowl mix all ingredients together until creamy. Pour into greased dish and cook for [a] 4½-5 minutes. Leave for a few minutes before turning out of dish.

	500 watt		650 watt/2 power
a	7 minutes (turn once)	a	6 minutes
	650 watt		
	a	PL.9 for 6 minutes	

Gingerbread

Cooking container: 7" round deep dish
Cooking time: 8-9 minutes
Number of servings: 6-8

3 oz. (75 g) margarine
6 oz. (175 g) black treacle
2 oz. (50 g) soft dark brown sugar
4 fl. oz. (120 ml) milk
½ teaspoon (2.5 ml) bicarbonate of soda
6 oz. (175 g) self raising flour
1 teaspoon (5 ml) ground ginger
good pinch mixed spice
1 size 2 egg beaten

Place the margarine, treacle, sugar and milk into a bowl and heat in the oven for [a] 3 minutes. Sprinkle in the bicarbonate of soda. Sift flour and spices together and add the milk mix and egg to the dry ingredients. Mix until smooth. Pour the mixture into the greased dish. Cook for [b] 5-6 minutes or until cake comes away from side of the dish. Cool on wire rack.

	500 watt		650 watt/2 power
a	4 minutes	a	3 minutes
b	9 minutes turn once	b	5-6 minutes
	650 watt		
	a	PL.9 for 2¾ minutes	
	b	PL.6 for 9-10 minutes	

Cheese Cake

Cooking container: 8" pie dish
Cooking time: 18 minutes
Number of servings: 5-6

2 oz. (50 g) butter
4 oz. (100 g) crushed digestive biscuits
1 oz. (25 g) caster sugar

For the Filling
8 oz. (225 g) cream cheese
8 oz. (225 g) curd cheese
3 eggs
2 oz. (50 g) caster sugar
1 tablespoon (15 ml) lemon juice

Melt butter in 8" pie dish, mix in biscuits and sugar and press onto base of dish. Heat in oven for [a] 1 minute to set. Heat cream and curd cheese in oven until soft. Mix in all other ingredients and pour onto biscuit base. Cook for [b] 2 minutes on full power then [c] 15 minutes on defrost. Leave to cool and top with fruit as required. Suitable for freezing.

500 watt		650 watt/2 power	
a	2 minutes	a	1 minute
b	3 minutes	b	2 minutes
c	17 minutes	c	15 minutes on defrost

650 watt	
a	PL.8 for 1 minute
b	PL.9 for 1½ minutes
c	PL.4 fro 7-8 minutes

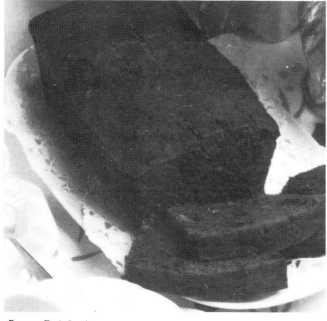

Banana Fruit Loaf

Chocolate Gateau

Cooking container: 7"-7½" round deep dish
Cooking time: 13 minutes
Number of servings: 6-8
6 oz. (175 g) soft dark brown sugar
8 oz. (225 g) butter
3 oz. (75 g) treacle
3 oz. (75 g) golden syrup
4 eggs
5 oz. (150 g) self raising flour
1 oz. (25 g) coconut, dessicated
2 oz. (50 g) cocoa

Line the base of dish and grease well. Cream the butter, sugar, treacle and syrup together. Slowly add the beaten eggs plus a tablespoon of flour. Beat well. Fold in the sifted cocoa and flour. Add the coconut. Pour the mixture into the dish. Cook in the oven for [a] 13 minutes. Turn cake out to cool. When cold, split and fill with cream. Decorate the top with cream and mandarin oranges.

500 watt		650 watt/2 power	
a	18-19 minutes turn twice	a	10-12 minutes

650 watt	
a	PL.6 for 12 minutes
	PL.9 for 3-4 minutes

Fruit and Banana Loaf

Cooking container: 2 lb loaf dish
Cooking time: 14 minutes
Number of servings: 10
10 oz. (275 g) mixed fruit
4 oz. (100 g) dark soft brown sugar
6 fl. oz. (180 ml) cold tea
1 banana, mashed
6 oz. (150 g) self raising flour
1 grade 2 egg, beaten

Put fruit and tea into bowl, heat for [a] 7 minutes and leave to stand until cool. Add flour, sugar, banana and egg. Mix well. Pour into greased loaf dish and cook for [b] 6-7 minutes. Leave to stand for 5 minutes before turning out.

500 watt		650 watt/2 power	
a	7-8 minutes	a	7 minutes
b	11 minutes	b	6-7 minutes

650 watt	
a	PL.9 for 6 minutes
b	PL.6 for 13 minute
	PL.9 for 2 minutes

Marmalade Cake

See colour plate page 147

Cooking container: 7"-7½" round deep dish
Cooking time: 13 minutes
Number of servings: 6-8

6 oz. (175 g) soft brown sugar
6 oz. (175 g) margarine
3 eggs, separated
1½ oz. (40 g) ground almonds
8½ oz. (240 g) self raising flour
3 level tablespoons (45 ml) chunky marmalade
2 oz. (50 g) chopped peel
grated rind and juice of orange
4 tablespoons (60 ml) water

Line the base of dish. Grease the sides and base well.
Cook the peel with 2 tablespoons of water in the oven for
[a] 2 mintues. Cream together the sugar and margarine.
Gradually add the egg yolks beating well. Stir in the
peel, orange rind and juice, water and marmalade. Fold
in the flour and almonds. Whisk the egg whites until
stiff and gently fold into the cake mix. Turn into the
baking dish and even out the top. Cook for [b] 11
minutes in the oven. The cake may be iced or left plain.
Store in airtight container.

	500 watt		650 watt/2 power
a	2½ minutes	a	1½ minutes
b	20 minutes	b	10-12 minutes
	turn once		
	650 watt		
a	PL.9 for 1½ minutes		
b	PL.6 for 11 minutes		
	PL.9 for 3-4 minutes		

Marmalade Cake

Orange Chocolate Marble Ring

Cooking container: Ring mould
Cooking time: 6½-7 minutes
Number of servings: 6-8

6 oz. (175 g) caster sugar
6 oz. (175 g) self raising flour
6 oz. (175 g) butter
3 eggs
4 tablespoons (60 ml) milk
2 tablespoons (30 ml) fresh orange juice
1 tablespoon (15 ml) cocoa

Mix the cocoa with 2 tablespoons of the milk until it
forms a smooth paste. Cream the butter with the sugar
until soft then beat in the eggs one at a time, fold in the
flour and 2 tablespoons of milk. Divide the mixture into
two separate containers, fold into one the orange juice
and into the other container fold the cocoa and milk.
Grease the ring mould and sprinkle with caster sugar.
Place spoonfuls of the two mixtures into the mould then
carefully swirl the mixtures. Cook in the oven for [a]
6½-7 minutes, allow to stand for 5 minutes before
turning out.

	500 watt		650 watt/2 power
a	8 minutes	a	6-7 minutes
	650 watt		
a	PL.6 for 8 minutes		
	PL.9 for 3 minutes		

Syrup Tart

Cooking container: 8" flan or pie dish
Cooking time: 4 minutes
Number of servings: 6-8

1 pre-cooked pastry flan case (see page 44)

2 oz. (50 g) white breadcrumbs
5 tablespoons (75 ml) golden syrup
grated rind of lemon
Cooked pastry fleurons

Mix the breadcrumbs with the syrup and the lemon.
Spread into pastry case. Decorate with fleurons. Cook
for [a] 4 minutes. Serve hot or cold.

	500 watt		650 watt/2 power
a	5 minutes	a	3½-4 minutes
	(turn once)		
	650 watt		
a	PL.9 for 3½-4 minutes		

Genoese Sponge

Cooking container: 7"-7½" round deep dish
Cooking time: 3½-4 minutes
Number of servings: 6
3 eggs
3 oz. (75 g) caster sugar
3 oz. (75 g) plain flour
pinch salt
1½ oz. (40 g) melted butter
Whisk the eggs with the sugar until volume has increased by 3 times. Fold in with a metal spoon very carefully the melted butter, sifted flour and salt. Turn into a greased baking dish and cook for approximately [a] 3½-4 minutes. Stand the cake in a dish for a few minutes before turning out onto a cooling rack. The cake can be cut into two halves and used as required. This cake could also be cooked in a shallow square dish or a shallow oblong dish and then cut into small cakes and iced individually.

500 watt		650 watt/2 power	
a	4½-5 minutes	a	3-4 minutes
650 watt			
a	PL.6 for 4 minutes		
	PL.9 for 1½-2 minutes		

Walnut Cake

Cooking container: 7" round deep dish
Cooking time: 7 minutes
Number of servings: 6
6 oz. (175 g) margarine
6 oz. (175 g) soft brown sugar
3 grade 3 eggs beaten
3 oz. (75 g) chopped walnuts
1 teaspoon (5 ml) vanilla essence
2 tablespoons (30 ml) milk
8 oz. (225 g) plain flour
1½ teaspoons (7.5 ml) baking powder
½ teaspoon (2.5 ml) salt
Cream together sugar and margarine until light and fluffy. Add eggs, one at a time and beat well. Add other ingredients and fold in with metal spoon. Line base of 7" dish with greaseproof paper, grease sides of dish and pour in mix. Cook for [a] 7 minutes. Stand for 5 minutes before turning out.

500 watt		650 watt/2 power	
a	14 minutes	a	6-7 minutes
	(turn once)		
650 watt			
a	PL.6 for 10 minutes		
	PL.9 for 1½ minutes		

Fruit Cake

Cooking container: 8" round deep dish
Cooking time: 30-33 minutes
Number of servings: 10-12

6 oz. (150 g) butter or margarine
6 oz. (150 g) dark soft brown sugar
5 oz. (125 g) currants
5 oz. (125 g) raisins
6 oz. (150 g) sultanas
4 grade 3 eggs, beaten
4 oz. (100 g) plain flour
5 oz. (125 g) self raising flour
1 level teaspoon (5 ml) ground nutmeg
1 level teaspoon (5 ml) ginger
4 oz. (100 g) glace cherries, chopped
2 oz. (50 g) ground almonds
1 tablespoon (15 ml) black treacle
2 tablespoons (30 ml) milk

Put all the fruit in a bowl, cover with cold water and cook for [a] 10 minutes. Leave to stand for 10 minutes then drain well. Cream the butter and sugar, add the eggs slowly continuing to cream. Fold in sieved flours, nutmeg, ground ginger and ground almonds. Add the fruit, chopped cherries, black treacle and milk. Stir gently until well mixed. Grease the dish and put greaseproof paper in the base. Put the mixture into the dish and level the surface. Cook for [b] 20-23 minutes. Leave to stand for 5 minutes before turning out.

500 watt		650 watt/2 power	
a	10 minutes	a	10 minutes
b	27-28 minutes	b	22-22½ minutes
	(turn twice)		
650 watt			
a	PL.9 for 10 minutes		
b	PL.5 for 30 minutes		

Butter Crisps

See colour plate page 147

Cooking container: Greaseproof paper
Cooking time: 2½ minutes
Number of servings: 30

5 oz. (150 g) butter
2 oz. (50 g) soft brown sugar
2 oz. (50 g) caster sugar
2 egg yolks (grade 4)
8 oz. (225 g) plain flour
4 teaspoons (20 ml) water

Cream the butter and sugars until light and fluffy. Beat in egg yolks then add flour and water working to a dough. Roll out on a very lightly floured board about ½" thick and cut using a pastry cutter about 2" in diameter. Place a circle of greaseproof paper on the turntable and place six biscuits in a circle onto it. Cook for [a] 2-2½ minutes or until set. Place onto kitchen paper on a rack to cool. Using the same piece of greaseproof paper continue to cook the rest of the biscuits. Makes about 2½ dozen.

	500 watt		650 watt/2 power
a	2½ minutes (turn once)	a	2-2½ minutes
	650 watt		
	a	PL.9 for 2-2½ minutes	

Selection of biscuits

Pineapple Raisin Cake

Cooking container: 7"-7½" round deep dish
Cooking time: 10 minutes
Number of servings: 8-10

6 oz. (175 g) self raising flour
3 oz. (75 g) glace cherries, chopped
1 x 8 oz. (225 g) tin pineapple
4 oz. (100 g) butter
3 oz. (75 g) dark soft brown sugar
3 eggs
8 oz. (225 g) raisins
3 tablespoons (45 ml) pineapple juice

Grease the dish, put greaseproof paper in base. Cream butter with the sugar, beat in the eggs one at a time. Fold in the chopped cherries, chopped pineapple and raisins. Fold in the flour and liquid. Place into dish, even out and microwave for [a] 10 minutes leaving dish for 5 minutes before turning out.

	500 watt		650 watt/2 power
a	16-18 minutes turn twice	a	9-10 minutes
	650 watt		
	a	PL.6 for 18 minutes	

Microwave Meringues

Cooking container: Paper cases
Cooking time: 2 minutes
Number of servings: Approx. 30

1 egg white
8-10 oz. (225 g-300 g) icing sugar

Whip egg white until stiff. Fold in icing sugar to form a very stiff mix. Place one flat teaspoon of mix into paper case. Cook 6 to 7 meringues for approximately [a] 2 minutes or until meringues do not "fall" when oven door is opened.

	500 watt		650 watt/2 power
a	2½-3 minutes	a	1½-2 minutes
	650 watt		
	a	PL.9 for 1½-2 minutes	

To make a complete topping for a pie:
Roll mix into ¾" diameter balls and place evenly over top of filling. Cook for approximately [a] 3-4 minutes or until set when oven door is opened.

	500 watt		650 watt/2 power
a	4-5 minutes	a	3-4 minutes
	650 watt		
	a	PL.9 for 3-4 minutes	

Victoria Sandwich

Cooking container: 7"-7½" round deep dish
Cooking time: 5 minutes
Number of servings: 6

6 oz (175 g) butter
6 oz (175 g) caster sugar
3 grade 3 eggs, beaten
6 oz (175 g) self raising flour
½ teaspoon vanilla essence
2 tablespoons (30 ml) warm water
½ teaspoon (2.5 ml) baking powder

Cream the butter or margarine until soft, add the sugar and beat well together until light and fluffy. Add the eggs gradually beating well after each addition. Sift the flour and baking powder and fold into the creamed mixture. Add the warm water and vanilla essence and fold in carefully. Turn mixture into the greased round cake dish and cook in the microwave oven for [a] 5 minutes. Leave to stand for 5 minutes in the cake dish before turning out onto a cooling rack. When cold, cut in half and sandwich the two halves together with jam or butter cream, dust the top with icing sugar.

	500 watt		650 watt/2 power
a	Approx. 8 minutes (turn once)	a	6 minutes
	650 watt		
	a	PL.9 for 7 minutes	

Individual Sponge Cakes with a selection of toppings

Simnel Cake (the traditional Easter Cake)

Cooking container: 8" round deep dish
Cooking time: 17½ minutes
Number of servings: 8-10

6 oz. (175 g) butter
6 oz. (175 g) dark brown sugar
3 standard eggs
8 oz. (225 g) self raising flour
½ teaspoon (2.5 ml) cinnamon
½ teaspoon (2.5 ml) nutmeg
1 lb (450 g) mixed fruit
3 tablespoons (45 ml) milk
12 oz. (350 g) almond paste

Place fruit in dish and cover with water. Cook for approximately [a] 3½ minutes to soften fruit. Strain and dry well, then mix in the flour. Cream butter and sugar and beat in eggs one at a time. Sieve flour and add cinnamon and nutmeg. Fold into egg mixture alternating with fruit. Add milk and mix to a soft consistency. Place two thirds of the mixture into a 8" greased dish with greaseproof paper on the base. Cover with thin rounds of marzipan made with 6 oz. almond paste. Cover with remaining mixture and cook for [b] 14 minutes. Leave to cool before turning out. Decorate top with remaining almond paste.
NB. Do not allow this cake to stand for too long before cooking.

	500 watt		650 watt/2 power
a	4 minutes	a	3 minutes
b	20 minutes	b	14 minutes
	650 watt		
	a	PL.9 for 3 minutes	
	b	PL.6 for 14 minutes	
		PL.9 for 5-6 minutes	

Individual Sponge Cakes

These can be made using the Victoria Sandwich recipe or a packet cake mix.
Put the mixture into one paper case placed inside another. Place the cases in the oven in a bun tray or into a ring shape. Cook 6 at a time for [a] 1-1½ minutes. Decorate as required when cool.

	500 watt		650 watt/2 power
a	1½-2 minutes	a	1-1½ minutes
	650 watt		
	a	PL.9 for 1-1½ minutes	

Microwave Florentines

Cooking Container: Grease proof paper
Cooking time: 3¼ minutes
Number of servings: 12-15

2 oz. (50 g) glace cherries
3 oz. (75 g) walnuts
1 oz. (25 g) sultanas
1 oz. (25 g) blanched whole almonds
1 oz. (25 g) chopped mixed peel
1 oz. (25 g) plain flour
2 oz. (50 g) butter
2 oz. (50 g) demerara sugar
1 tablespoon (15 ml) syrup

Melt the butter, sugar and syrup together in the oven for [a] 1½ minutes. Chop the cherries, walnuts, almonds and sultanas. Add with the mixed peel and flour to the liquid. Place teaspoons of the mix well apart on the greased paper in the oven. Cook for [b] 1¾ minutes. Remove from the oven and shape edges neatly with the side of a fork. When slightly cooled, lift carefully on to cooling rack. When cooked, the florentines can be coated with melted chocolate on one side.

	500 watt		650 watt/2 power	
a	2 minutes	a	1-1½ minutes	
b	3 minutes	b	1½ minutes	
	650 watt			
	a	PL.8 for 1½ minutes		
	b	PL.6 for 2¼ minutes		

Flapjacks

See colour plate page 147
Cooking container: 8" shallow round dish
Cooking time: 5 minutes
Number of servings: 8-12
4 oz. (100 g) butter
1 oz. (25 g) white sugar
1½ oz. (40 g) soft brown sugar
4 level tablespoons (60 ml) golden syrup
8 oz. (225 g) rolled oats
pinch salt

Place the butter and sugar into a bowl and put in the oven for 1-1½ minutes, until the butter is melted. Stir in the syrup and salt, then work in the rolled oats until completely mixed. Press the mixture into a greased 8" shallow dish. Cook for [a] 5 minutes. Leave to cool in the dish and then cut into pieces.

	500 watt		650 watt/2 power	
a	6 minutes turn once	a	4½ minutes	
	650 watt			
	a	PL.9 for 4 minutes		

Shortbread

Cooking container: 7" shallow Round Dish
Cooking time: 4½ minutes
Number of servings: 6

4 oz. (100 g) butter
1 oz. (25 g) caster sugar
1 oz. (25 g) dark brown sugar
4 oz. (100 g) plain flour
2 oz. (50 g) cornflour

Sieve the cornflour and plain flour together. Cream the butter until soft and add the sugars and beat until the mixture is fluffy. Work in the flour. Roll up to a ball and roll out to about 7" in diameter using as little flour as possible. Grease the container well and line base with greaseproof paper. Microwave for [a] 4½ minutes. Leave to stand for 1 hour until cool.

	500 watt		650 watt/2 power	
a	5½ minutes	a	4-5 minutes	
	650 watt			
	a	PL.9 for 4-5 minutes		

Ginger Crisps

See colour plate page 147
Cooking container: Greaseproof paper
Cooking time: 1½ minutes
Number of servings:15-20

4 oz. (100 g) butter
1 level tablespoon (15 ml) golden syrup
6 oz. (175 g) self raising flour
1 level teaspoon (5 ml) ground ginger
pinch of bicarbonate of soda
3 oz. (75 g) caster sugar

Sieve together flour, ginger, bicarbonate of soda and add sugar and leave to one side. In a bowl melt the butter with the golden syrup for [a] 1 minute. Stir the dry ingredients into the syrup and butter mix. Place in refrigerator for 2 hours. Roll a teaspoon of the mixture into a ball, place on greaseproof paper in a circle in the microwave oven. Cook six at a time for [b] 1½ minutes or until set. Place onto a rack to cool before storing in a tin.

	500 watt		650 watt/2 power
a	2 minutes	a	45 seconds
b	2 minutes	b	1 minute

	650 watt
a	PL.8 for 1 minute
b	PL.6 for 2 minutes or until set

Coconut Raspberry Buns

Cooking container: Bun tray
Cooking time: 6 minutes
Number of servings: 18

6 oz. (175 g) self raising flour
2 oz. (50 g) coconut flour (or dessicated coconut)
4 oz. (100 g) margarine
pinch salt
4 oz. (100 g) sugar
1 egg
milk

For the Topping
Dessicated coconut
Raspberry jam

Rub the fat into the flour mixed with salt and coconut. Mix in sugar. Make a well in centre, pour in beaten egg and mix in dry ingredients adding milk as required. Mixture should be a soft dropping consistency. Place a heaped teaspoonful of mixture into each bun case. Place the cases into bun tray or on to base of oven (six at a time in a circle) and cook for approximately [a] 2 minutes until set. Place bun cases onto cooling rack. Cook each batch and allow to cool. Spread the tops of buns with a little warm raspberry jam and sprinkle with coconut before serving.

	500 watt		650 watt/2 power
a	2½-3 minutes	a	1½-2 minutes

	650 watt
a	PL.9 for 1½-2 minutes

Chocolate Crispies

Cooking container: 2½ pint bowl
Cooking time: 3 minutes.
Number of servings: 12

1 oz. (25 g) sugar
1 oz. (25 g) cocoa
2 cups of cornflakes
2 oz. (50 g) margarine
1 tablespoon (15 ml) golden syrup

Place sugar, margarine and golden syrup into 2½ pint bowl. Heat for approx. [a] 3 minutes. Mix in cocoa and then stir in cornflakes. Place in cases and allow to cool.

	500 watt		650 watt/2 power
a	3-4 minutes	a	2½ minutes

	650 watt
a	PL.8 for 3 minutes

Lemon Sponge

Cooking container: Loaf dish
Cooking time: 7¼ minutes
Number of servings: 8-10

4 oz. (100 g) margarine
3½ oz. (90 g) caster sugar
5 oz. (125 g) self raising flour
1 level teaspoon (5 ml) baking powder
2 grade 2 eggs beaten
2 tablespoons (30 ml) lemon curd
2 tablespoons (30 ml) warm water
3 tablespoons (45 ml) lemon juice
2 tablespoons (30 ml) caster sugar

Cream the margarine and 3½ oz caster sugar, then add the eggs slowly while still beating. Add a tablespoon of sifted flour with the eggs, then fold in the rest of the flour and baking powder. Put the 2 tablespoons of lemon curd into a small basin and cook for [a] 45 seconds, stir, add the water then add this to the cake mix. Grease and line the base of a 1 lb loaf dish and add cake mixture. Cook for about [b] 6-6½ minutes. Leave to stand for 5 minutes then turn out onto serving dish. Pour the lemon juice over the top and dredge with caster sugar.

	500 watt		650 watt/2 power
a	1 minute	a	30 seconds
b	6-7 minutes (turn once)	b	5-6 minutes

	650 watt
a	PL.9 for 45 seconds
b	PL.9 for 5-6 minutes

Strawberry Shortcake

Cooking container: 8" flan dish
Cooking time: 5 minutes
Number of servings: 6-8

3 oz. (75 g) margarine
8 oz. (225 g) self raising flour
¾ teaspoon salt
3 oz. (75 g) caster sugar
3 tablespoons (75 g) milk
1 egg, beaten

Rub the fat into the flour and salt, until the mixture is like fine breadcrumbs. Stir in the sugar, add the egg a little at a time until the mix begins to bind. Stir in the milk, knead the mixture lightly into a smooth dough. Press the dough into an 8" flan dish. Cook for [a] 5 minutes. Turn out onto a cooling tray and leave to cool before cutting in half and filling with strawberries and cream.

	500 watt		650 watt/2 power
a	6½ minutes (turn once)	a	4½-5 minutes
	650 watt		
a	PL.6 for 5 minutes PL.9 for 1½-2 minutes		

Apple and Almond Cake

Cooking container: 7"-7½" deep dish
Cooking time: 8 minutes
Number of servings: 8-10

3 oz. (75 g) soft margarine
3 oz. (75 g) soft dark brown sugar
1 tablespoon (15 ml) golden syrup
2 oz. (50 g) ground almonds
4 oz. (100 g) sultanas
4 oz. (100 g) self raising flour, sieved
½ teaspoon (2.5 ml) cinnamon
1 x 5 oz. prepared and chopped cooking apple.
3 grade 4 eggs
3 tablespoons (45 ml) milk

Place all ingredients into mixing bowl and mix until smooth. Grease and line dish. Pour in mix and cook for [a] 8 minutes.

	500 watt		650 watt/2 power
a	12-14 minutes turn twice	a	7 minutes
	650 watt		
a	PL.6 for 12 minutes PL.9 for 1½-2 minutes		

Bread

Cooking container: Greased loaf dish
Cooking time: 5 minutes
Number of servings: 8-12

1 teaspoon (5 g) dried yeast
1 teaspoon (5 g) sugar
knob of margarine
½ pint (275 ml) warm water
½ lb (225 g) wholemeal flour
2 teaspoons (10 g) salt
2 teaspoons (10 g) black treacle
½ lb (225 g) strong white flour

Put yeast, sugar, margarine and water into bowl and leave until frothy (5-10 minutes). Mix flour and salt together. Add treacle and yeast mixture to flour and knead into soft dough. Put into greased loaf dish, brush top with milk and sprinkle with sesame or sunflower seeds. Prove by microwaving, 15 seconds approximately then rest for a couple of minutes. Repeat this process until dough has risen twice its size. Microwave for [a] 5 minutes until top is just firm. Brown top under grill. Turn out of container and leave edges to dry.

	500 watt		650 watt/2 power
a	7½-8½ minutes	a	4¾ minutes
	650 watt		
a	PL.9 for 4¾ minutes		

Bread

Jams Preserves and Sweets

Jams Preserves and Sweets

Even though the time-saving is not great, the end result from cooking microwave cooked jams, preserves and sweets is so good they are worth trying. The cooking container is easier to clean too!

As a general rule:
1 Use a large container.
2 Container must withstand boiling sugar.
3 Container will get hot so remove from oven with ovengloves.
4 Dissolve sugar completely before boiling.

Microwave method:
1 Place sugar and liquid into large container and heat gently stirring often to dissolve sugar.
2 When sugar is dissolved bring to boil.
3 Follow recipe.

Jars and suitable containers can be heated in the microwave oven by rinsing in clean water and placing six at a time in the oven until hot. Remove with ovengloves.

Rhubarb Jam

Cooking container: 4 pint casserole
Cooking time: 30 minutes
Makes: Approx. 1½ lb

1 lb (450 g) rhubarb, washed and cut into 1" pieces
1 lemon
1 orange
1 lb (450 g) sugar

Place rhubarb into a large casserole. Cover and cook for [a] 5-6 minutes. Meanwhile grate rind from lemon and orange. Squeeze and strain the juice from the lemon and the orange. Tie the pips in a scrap of cheesecloth. Add the rind, juice, pips and sugar to the cooked rhubarb. Stir well. cook, stirring regularly for [b] 20-25 minutes or until thick and will gel on a cold plate. Pot and cover.

	500 watt		650 watt/2 power
a	10-12 minutes	a	5 minutes
b	20-25 minutes	b	20-25 minutes
	650 watt		
	a	PL.9 for 5 minutes	
	b	PL.8 for 35 minutes	

Spring Jam

Cooking container: 7 pint dish
Cooking time: 35-40 minutes
Makes: 1 lb

1 stick (8 oz) rhubarb chopped
½ lb (225 g) dried apricots
2 lb (900 g) granulated sugar
1 pint (568 ml) water/juice mixed

Soak dried apricots overnight or place in microwave, pour boiling water over apricots and microwave for [a] 3 minutes. Leave to stand for 5 minutes. Cook rhubarb with no extra water for [b] 2 minutes or until soft. Drain apricots placing drained juice into a 1 pint jug. Cook apricots for [c] 5 minutes until tender. Put sugar with apricots and rhubarb. Stir and add apricot juice made up to 1 pint with boiling water. Place bowl back into oven and bring to boil — approx. [d] 10 minutes. Stir. Cook for another [e] 10 minutes and check temperature with thermometer. If setting point is not reached continue cooking in 5 minute bursts until setting point is reached. Sterilize jars, pots and cover.

500 watt		650 watt/2 power	
Not suitable	a	3 minutes	
	b	2 minutes	
	c	5 minutes	
	d	10 minutes	
	e	8 minutes	
650 watt			
a	PL.9 for 3 minutes		
b	PL.9 for 2 minutes		
c	PL.7 for 5 minutes		
d	PL.7 for 10 minutes		
e	PL.7 for 10 minutes		

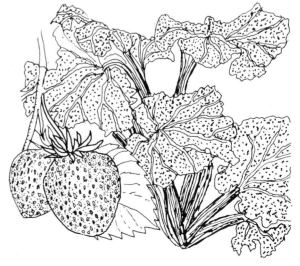

Marmalade

Cooking container: 7 pint dish
Cooking time: 2 hours 3 minutes
Makes: 6 lb

2 lb (900 g) seville oranges
1 lemon
3½ lb (1.6 kilo) sugar
3 pints (1.7 litre) water

Heat whole fruit in oven for [a] 3 minutes. Cut in half and squeeze out juice. Save pips and wrap in muslin. Slice skin finely and place skin, juice and pips into a large 7 pint dish. Add water and heat for [b] 1 hour. Stir occasionally. Stir in sugar until dissolved then return to oven for another [c] 1 hour. Remove any scum and pour into sterilized jars.
Note: Peel must be cut fairly finely and marmalade must be stirred. Sugar must also be well dissolved before second boiling.

500 watt		650 watt/2 power	
Not suitable		a	2½ minutes
		b	50-60 minutes
		c	50-60 minutes
650 watt			
a	PL.9 for 2½ minutes		
b	PL.9 for 50 minutes		
c	PL.8 for 60 minutes		

Strawberry Jam

Cooking container: 4 pint casserole
Cooking time: 19 minutes
Makes: 2 lb of jam

1 lb (450 g) fresh strawberries, prepared
1 fl. oz. (30 ml) lemon juice
1 lb (450 g) caster sugar

Cook fruit and lemon juice in the microwave oven for [a] 4 minutes then beat to a pulp with a wooden spoon. Add sugar stirring well. Cook for [b] 4 minutes until sugar has dissolved and stir again. Cook for a further [c] 11 minutes stirring once during cooking cycle and again at the end of the cooking cycle.
Note: Jam sets well when left to cool.

500 watt		650 watt/2 power	
a	5 minutes	a	3½ minutes
b	5 minutes	b	3½-4 minutes
c	14 minutes	c	10 minutes
650 watt			
a	PL.8 for 4 minutes		
b	PL.8 for 4 minutes		
c	PL.9 for 10 minutes		

Lemon Curd

Cooking container: 4 pint casserole
Cooking time: 12 minutes
Makes: Approx. 2 lb of lemon curd

1 lb (450 g) caster sugar
4 eggs
juice of 3 lemons
grated rind of 1 lemon
¼ lb (100 g) butter

The lemons will yield more juice and zest if heated in the microwave before squeezing for approximately 1 minute. Put sugar, butter, juice and rind of lemon into a cooking container and cook for [a] 8 minutes stirring frequently. During this time the sugar should dissolve and come to a rolling boil. Add the well beaten eggs, return to oven and stir frequently until mixture thickens [b] (approx. 4 minutes). Bottle in the usual way.

500 watt		650 watt/2 power	
a	12 minutes	a	7 minutes
b	5 minutes	b	4 minutes
	approx.		approx.
650 watt			
a	PL.7 for 10 minutes		
b	PL.7 for 6 minutes		
	approx.		

Raspberry Jam

Cooking container: 7 pint casserole
Cooking time: 24 minutes
Makes: 2 x 12 oz jars

1 lb (450 g) frozen raspberries
1 lb (450 g) caster sugar

Defrost and cook raspberries in oven for [a] 5 minutes. Stir in sugar and microwave for [b] 4 minutes then stir thoroughly. Cook for a further [c] 15 minutes but stirring after 10 minutes of the cooking time.
Note: Jam sets well when left to cool.

500 watt		650 watt/2 power	
a	7 minutes	a	4½ minutes
b	6 minutes	b	3½ minutes
c	18 minutes	c	15 minutes
650 watt			
a	PL.9 for 4½ minutes		
b	PL.7 for 6 minutes		
c	PL.9 for 15 minutes		

Beetroot Chutney

Cooking container: 7 pint casserole
Cooking time: 55 minutes
Makes: Approx. 6 lb

¼ lb (100 g) apples, peeled and chopped
2¼ lb (1 k) cooked beetroot, finely chopped
¾ lb (350 g) onions, finely chopped
1 tablespoon (5 ml) salt
½ lb (225 g) raisins
¾ pint (425 ml) malt vinegar
8 oz. (225 g) soft brown sugar
6 peppercorns
6 cloves
½ oz. (12.5 g) allspice

Place beetroot, apples and onion with salt, vinegar, raisins and sugar into a large dish. Wrap and tie up spices in muslin bag and place in dish, cook covered for [a] 30-35 minutes, stirring every 10 minutes until thick. Pour into jars and seal.

500 watt Not suitable	650 watt/2 power	
	a	8 minutes
	b	30-35 minutes

650 watt		
a	PL.9 for 8 minutes	
b	PL.7 for 35-40 minutes	

Apple Chutney

Cooking container: 7 pint casserole
Cooking time: 2 hours
Makes: Approx. 6 lb

3 lb (1.4 k) cooking apples, peeled, cored and chopped
3 lb (1.4 k) onions, peeled and chopped
2 lemons
1½ lb (675 g) demerara sugar
1 pint (600 ml) malt vinegar
6 cloves
1 lb (450 g) sultanas

Heat onions and apples covered for [a] 5 minutes. Add juice and rind of lemons and stir in all other ingredients. Cook uncovered for [b] 1½-2 hours, stirring occasionally until thick. Pour into sterilized jars and cover.

500 watt Not suitable	650 watt/2 power	
	a	4 minutes
	b	1½-2 hours

650 watt		
a	PL.9 for 4 minutes	
b	PL.9 for 1½-2 hours	

Plum Chutney

Cooking container: 7 pint casserole
Cooking time: 1 hour 40 minutes
Makes: Approx. 6 lb

2 lb (900 g) plums, stoned and halved
1½ pints (900 ml) malt vinegar
2 lb (900 g) soft brown sugar
¾ lb (300 g) finely chopped onions
2 cloves finely chopped garlic
1 lb (450 g) sultanas
2 teaspoons (10 ml) dried mustard
2 level tablespoons (30 ml) ground ginger
1 level tablespoon (15 ml) ground allspice
2 oz. (50 g) salt
grated rind of orange

Heat vinegar and sugar in large container for [a] 10 minutes. Stir to dissolve sugar. Add plums and cook for [b] 22 minutes. Add all other ingredients and cook for [c] 1 hour 20 minutes stirring occasionally. Pour into warm jars, cover and seal.

500 watt Not suitable	650 watt/2 power	
	a	8 minutes
	b	20 minutes
	c	1 hour 10 minutes

650 watt		
a	PL.7 for 10 minutes	
b	PL.9 for 20 minutes	
c	PL.9 for 1 hour 10 minutes	

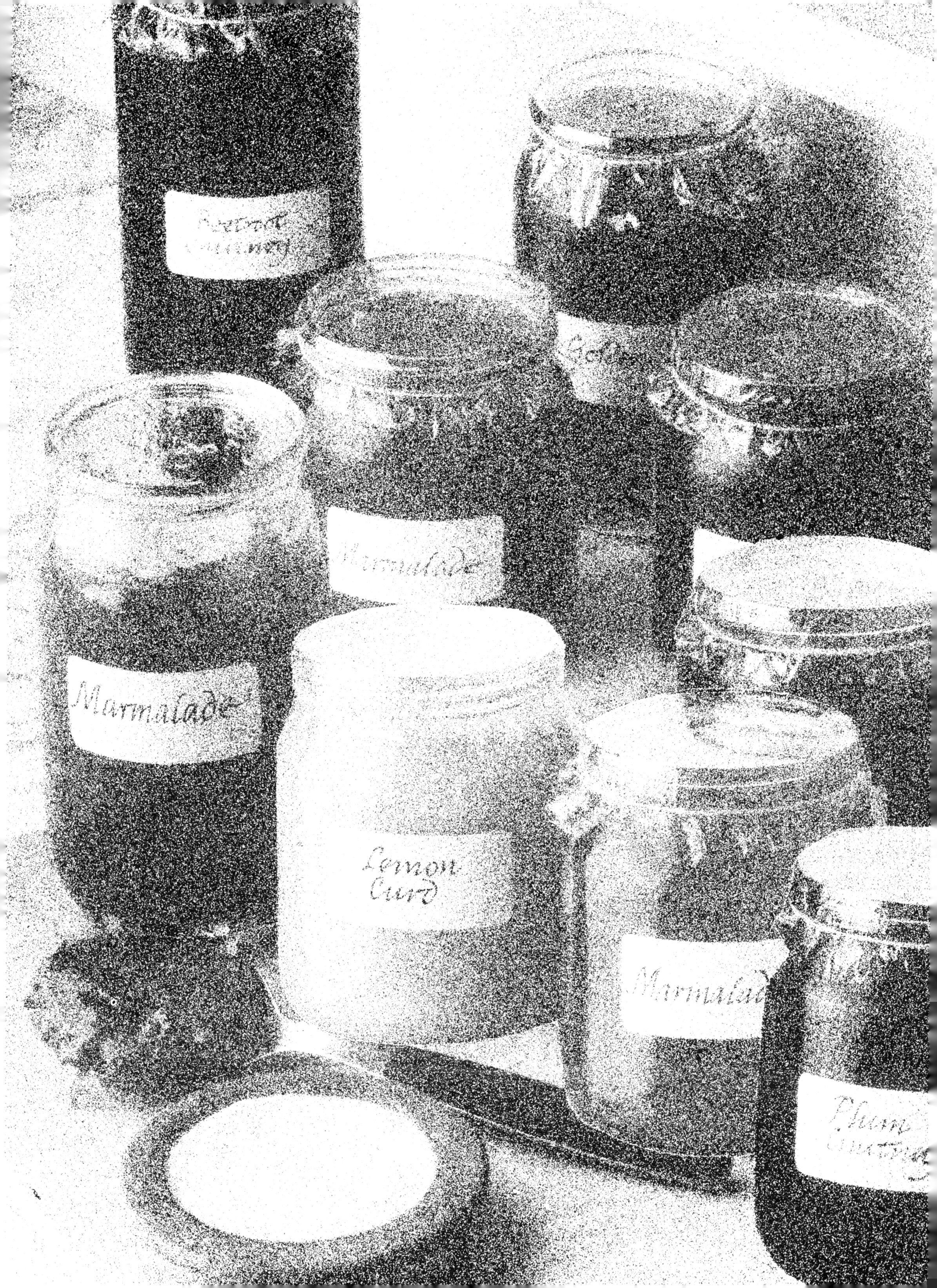
Marmalade
Lemon Curd

Cider & Sage Jelly

Cooking container: 7 pint casserole
Cooking time: 24 minutes
Makes: Approx. 2½ lb

4 tablespoons (60 ml) chopped fresh sage
¾ pint (450 ml) sweet cider
2 lb (900 g) sugar
¼ pint (150 ml) liquid pectin
¼ pint (150 ml) water

Heat water to boil in the microwave oven. Add the sage to the water and let it stand for 15 minutes. Heat the sugar and cider in a large container for [a] 10 minutes — stirring once during cycle. Ensure that sugar is dissolved. Strain herbs and add the water to the cider. Heat in oven until boiling [b] approx. 8 minutes. Stir in the liquid pectin. Heat for [c] 3 minutes, stir and stand for 1 minute. Skim the surface and pour into jars.

	500 watt		650 watt/2 power
a	13 minutes	a	8½ minutes
b	10 minutes approx.	b	6 minutes
c	3½ minutes	c	3 minutes

	650 watt
a	PL.7 for 14 minutes
b	PL.9 for 6 minutes
c	PL.9 for 3 minutes

Coconut Ice

See colour plate page 163

Cooking container: 7 pint bowl
Cooking time: 12-13 minutes
Makes: Approx. 1¼ lbs.

1 lb (450 g) caster sugar
¼ pint (150 ml) milk
3 oz. (75 g) dessicated coconut
cochineal

Butter a shallow tray or dish (approx. 7" x 9" x 1"). Dissolve sugar in milk for [a] 5 minutes, stirring occasionally. Bring to boil until the soft ball stage is reached, approx [b] 7-8 minutes or 240°F. Stir in the coconut and pour half the mix into the tray, spreading it evenly. Colour the remainder a pale pink with the cochineal and pour over. Leave to set then cut into one inch squares. (Try using 6 oz shredded coconut instead of dessicated for an even tastier result).

	500 watt		650 watt/2 power
a	8 minutes	a	4-5 minutes
b	12 minutes	b	4-6 minutes

	650 watt
a	PL.6 for 7 minutes
b	PL.9 for 4-6 minutes

Pickled Beetroot

Cooking container: Casserole dish
Cooking time: 17-20 minutes
Makes: Approx. 1½-2 lbs.

1 lb (450 g) beetroot
4 tablespoons (60 ml) water
1 teaspoon (5 ml) pickling spices
2 oz. (50 g) sugar
2½ tablespoons (45 ml) cider vinegar

Wash and cut the top and bottom of the beetroot, cut in half if large. Put into casserole dish, add one tablespoon of water and cover. Cook for [a] 12-15 minutes and allow to stand for 10 minutes. Remove the beetroot peel, slice and leave to one side. To the remaining liquid add the rest of the ingredients and stir well. Cook covered for [b] 5 minutes until liquid boils. Stir once during cooking cycle. Leave to cool. Put the beetroot into 1 lb jars, strain the vinegar mixture on top and cover. Will keep in the refrigerator for about 5-6 weeks.

500 watt		650 watt/2 power
Not suitable	a	10-12 minutes
	b	4 minutes

	650 watt
a	PL.9 for 10-12 minutes
b	PL.9 for 4 minutes

Chocolate Truffles

See colour plate page 163

Cooking container: 2 pint bowl
Cooking time: 2 minutes
Number of servings: Approximately 15

3 oz. (75 g) plain chocolate
½ oz. (15 g) butter
1 teaspoon (5 ml) rum
1 teaspoon (5 ml) cream
1 oz. (25 g) sponge cake crumbs

Melt chocolate in bowl with butter for [a] 2 minutes. Stir halfway during heating time and on removal from the oven. Stir in rum, cream and cake crumbs. Allow mixture to cool slightly then roll into 15 individual balls. To decorate roll the truffles in drinking chocolate or chocolate vermicelli and place into small paper cases.

	500 watt		650 watt/2 power
a	2-2½ minutes stir every 30 seconds	a	1½ minutes

	650 watt
a	PL.7 for 2 minutes

Jams, Preserves and Chutneys P.161

Toffee Apples

Cooking container: 4 pint casserole
Cooking time: 17-19 minutes
Makes: 8

8 small apples
8 oz. (225 g) demerara sugar
1 tablespoon (15 ml) golden syrup
1 oz. (25 g) butter
2 tablespoons (30 ml) vinegar
5 tablespoons (75 ml) water

Dissolve the sugar with the water, syrup, butter and vinegar in the microwave oven for [a] 7 minutes, stirring frequently. Bring to the boil and continue heating until the toffee reaches the "crack" stage, approx. [b] 10-12 minutes. (To check when the toffee has reached this point, drop into a small amount of cold water. If it hardens immediately, but can be cracked, the toffee is ready). Dip apples into toffee and stand them on buttered greaseproof paper to set. If you wish to put them in the refrigerator, wait until the toffee is hard.

	500 watt		650 watt/2 power
a	17½ minutes	a	6 minutes
b	15 minutes approx.	b	8-10 minutes

	650 watt	
a	PL.7 for 9 minutes	
b	PL.8 for 10-12 minutes	

Chocolate Fudge

Cooking container: 7 pint casserole
Cooking time: Approx. 21 minutes
Makes: Approx 1 lb

1 lb..(450 g) caster sugar
2 oz. butter
1 large tin evaporated milk
4 oz. (100 g) plain chocolate

Use the same size greased tray or dish as for Coconut Ice. Heat sugar, milk and butter in a large casserole for [a] 5 minutes, stirring to dissolve sugar. Boil until the soft ball stage is reached, stirring occasionally approx [b] 16 minutes or 240°F. Add chocolate and beat until thick and creamy. Pour into tray and leave to set. Cut into one inch squares and wrap in waxed paper.

500 watt		650 watt/2 power	
Not suitable		a	5 minutes
		b	15 minutes approx.

	650 watt	
a	PL.9 for 5 minutes	
b	PL.9 for 15 minutes approx.	

Honey Fruit Nut Caramel

Cooking container: 7 pint casserole
Cooking time: 7½ minutes
Makes: 15-20

3 oz. (45 g) butter
5 oz. (150 g) golden syrup
6 oz. (175 g) clear honey
4 oz. (100 g) walnut halves
4 oz. (100 g) stoned dates

Grease and line shallow dish (approx. 9" x 7" x 1"). Melt butter for [a] 1½ minutes then add syrup and honey. Bring to boil for [b] 2 minutes then boil for a further [c] 5-6 minutes (or until 250°F is reached). Meanwhile chop walnuts and dates finely. Remove hot mixture, add dates and nuts. Beat vigorously until opaque in colour. Pour into tin and leave to cool. Cut into one inch squares. Wrap in wax paper when set.

	500 watt		650 watt/2 power
a	2 minutes	a	1½ minutes
b	4 minutes	b	2 minutes
c	6 minutes	c	5-6 minutes

	650 watt	
a	PL.9 for 1½ minutes	
b	PL.9 for 2 minutes	
c	PL.9 for 5-6 minutes	

Collettes

Cooking container: 2 pint bowl
Cooking time: 1½ minutes
Makes: 18

9 oz. (250 g) plain chocolate
4 tablespoons (60 ml) strong black coffee
2 oz. (50 g) butter
2 egg yolks
rum essence
hazelnuts

Break 4 oz chocolate into a basin and heat until melted [a] 1½ minutes. Put one teaspoon of chocolate in a small paper case. Press another case over the chocolate to squeeze the chocolate up the sides. Repeat with remaining chocolate and leave to set. Peel off the paper cases. Melt the remaining chocolate and mix with coffee. When cool beat in butter, egg yolks and rum to taste. Leave to thicken. Pipe this mixture into the chocolate cases, top with a hazelnut and leave to set.

	500 watt		650 watt/2 power
a	1½-2 minutes	a	1-2 minutes

	650 watt	
a	PL.7 for 1½-2 minutes	

Notes:

Recipes	Page No:	My Timing	Recipes	Page No:	My Timing

Meals in Minutes

Meals in Minutes

The microwave oven is one of the simplest ways of cooking food. This chapter includes a selection of easy to make dishes, most of which are ideal for children to prepare in the oven with a little assistance from Mum.

Many of the ingredients used in the recipes are taken from the store cupboard or the freezer, showing how quick and easy it is to prepare a dish at short notice. See defrost section for any frozen foods you wish to use.

Meatball Stew

Cooking container: Roasting rack,
3 pint casserole dish

Cooking time: 23 minutes
Number of servings: 6

1 lb (450 g) minced beef
1 egg
2½ oz. (60 g) brown breadcrumbs
10 oz. (283 g) can sliced carrots
10 oz. (283 g) can garden peas
10 oz. (283 g) can new potatoes
10 oz. (283 g) can condensed tomato soup
10 oz. (283 g) can condensed beef broth
1 teaspoon (5 ml) minced onion
salt and pepper

Combine beef, breadcrumbs and egg, season well. Make into 10 balls, place in a circle on a roasting rack and cook or [a] 8 minutes. Mix drained vegetables and soup in a 3 pint casserole dish. Add meatballs and meat juices. Heat covered for [b] 15 minutes. Canned meatballs can be used if there is no time to make your own. If you do this, omit the beef broth from the recipe.

	500 watt		650 watt/2 power
a	12 minutes	a	7 minutes
b	20 minutes	b	13 minutes
	650 watt		
	a	PL.7 for 10 minutes	
	b	PL.8 for 14 minutes	

Temp Probe: **b** 85°C, PL.8

Chicken Casserole

Cooking container: 3 pint casserole
Cooking time: 42 minutes or 34 minutes without vegetables
Number of servings: 4
4 chicken portions (total weight approx. 2 lb)
1 can cook-in-sauce

Place 4 chicken portions into a dish and pour sauce over. Cover and cook for [a] 10 minutes on full power. Turn the oven to defrost power and cook for [b] 24 minutes. If adding cooked vegetables, turn the oven to full power for an additional [c] 8 minutes before serving.

	500 watt		650 watt/2 power
a	12 minutes	a	8 minutes
b	30 minutes on defrost	b	24 minutes
	650 watt		
	a	PL.9 for 8 minutes	
	b	PL.5 for 26 minutes	
	c	PL.9 for 7 minutes	

Chicken Casserole

Cod Portuguese

Cooking container: 3 pint dish
Cooking time: 17 minutes
Number of servings: 4

4 frozen cod steaks
1 sliced onion
1 sliced green pepper
6 stuffed olives
½ oz. (15 g) butter
1 can tomato soup
½ teaspoon (2.5 ml) oregano

Cook the sliced onion and pepper in the butter for [a] 5 minutes. Mix vegetables with the soup, olives and oregano. Pour over fish and cook covered for [b] 12 minutes.

	500 watt		650 watt/2 power	
a	6 minutes	a	4 minutes	
b	16 minutes	b	10 minutes	
	650 watt			
	a	PL.8 for 4 minutes		
	b	PL.9 for 10 minutes		

Juliette's Special Tea

Cooking container: 1½ pint dish
Cooking time: 5-7 minutes
Number of servings: 1

2 oz. (50 g) macaroni cooked
1 small tin frankfurters drained and sliced
small tin condensed mushroom soup

Mix all ingredients together in a 1½ pint dish. Heat in the microwave oven until piping hot approximately [a] 5-7 minutes. Serve with tomato sauce.

	500 watt		650 watt/2 power
a	7 minutes	a	4-5 minutes
	650 watt		
	a	PL.8 for 6 minutes	

Corn & Tuna Bake

Cooking container: 2 pint dish
Cooking time: 18 minutes
Number of servings: 4

7 oz. (200 g) can tuna fish drained
11½ oz. (326 g) can Mexicorn
7 oz. (200 g) can Mexicorn
3 eggs
½ pint (300 ml) milk
1 level tablespoon (15 ml) flour
salt and pepper
3 oz. (75 g) grated cheese
crushed crisps

Combine tuna and Mexicorn in a 2 pint dish. Mix eggs, milk and flour, stir this into the dish. Season lightly and sprinkle with cheese. Cook for [a] 3 minutes on full power then [b] 15 minutes on defrost until set. Sprinkle with crushed crisps before serving.

	500 watt		650 watt/2 power	
a	5 minutes	a	2½ minutes	
b	16 minutes	b	15 minutes	
	650 watt			
	a	PL.9 for 2½ minutes		
	b	PL.4 for 15 minutes		

Mushroom Scramble

Cooking container: 2 pint bowl
Cooking time: 4-4½ minutes
Number of servings: 2

1 Can Mushroom Omelette Mate
4 eggs
2 tablespoons (30 ml) milk

Combine all ingredients together in a 2 pint bowl or jug. Cook in the oven for [a] 2 minutes, stir and return to oven for [b] 2-2½ minutes. Stir and serve on hot buttered toast.

	500 watt		650 watt/2 power	
a	3 minutes	a	2 minutes	
b	3½ minutes	b	2-2½ minutes	
	650 watt			
	a	PL.7 for 2 minutes		
	b	PL.9 for 2-2½ minutes		

Fish Finger Scramble

Cooking container: Browning dish & 2 pint bowl
Cooking time: 5 minutes
Number of servings: 4-5

1 packet of 10 Fish Fingers
A little oil
½ oz. (15 g) butter
3 rashers bacon, chopped
2 oz. (50 g) mushrooms, chopped
4 eggs, beaten and seasoned
Parsley

Cook the Fish Fingers either as directed on the packet or in a browning dish in the microwave oven. Place the butter, bacon and mushrooms into a 2 pint bowl and cook in the oven for [a] 2 minutes. Add the eggs and cook for [b] 1½ minutes. Stir and cook until thick (approximately [c] 1½ minutes). Stir before serving with the Fish Fingers.

	500 watt		650 watt/2 power
a	3 minutes	a	1½ minutes
b	2 minutes	b	1½ minutes
c	2 minutes	c	1½ minutes approx.

	650 watt	
a	PL.7 for 2½ minutes	
b	PL.7 for 2 minutes	
c	PL.7 for aprrox. 2 minutes	

Ham Joint

See colour plate page 169

Cooking container: Roaster bag
Cooking time: 6 minutes
Number of servings: 3-4

1 lb (450 g) canned ham or bacon
1 small can of pineapple rings
1 tablespoon (15 ml) brown sugar
1 teaspoon (2.5 ml) prepared mustard
pinch of powdered ginger
Maraschino cherries

Place joint into roaster bag. Combine pineapple juice, sugar, mustard and ginger. Pour this over the ham in the bag and leave for at least one hour. Place bag in the oven and heat for [a] 6 minutes. Remove joint and garnish with pineapple rings and cherries and pour sauce over. Serve immediately.

	500 watt		650 watt/2 power
a	9 minutes	a	5 minutes

	650 watt	
a	PL.7 for 8 minutes	

Temp Probe: **a** 70°C, PL.7

Gammon Veronique

Cooking container: 2 pint bowl & roasting rack
Cooking time: 14-17 minutes
Number of servings: 4

10½ oz. (295 g) can condensed cream of chicken soup, undiluted
1 soup can white wine
1 small onion, finely chopped
4 oz. (100 g) grapes, sliced in half with pips removed
salt and pepper
4 gammon rashers

Heat onion in a 2 pint bowl in oven for [a] 1 minute. Add soup and wine, heat for [b] 4 minutes. Stir in grapes and seasoning. Place gammon steaks on roasting griddle and cook in oven for [c] 7-10 minutes (depending on size). Place on serving dish. Heat sauce for [d] 2 minutes, stir and pour over gammon steaks.

	500 watt		650 watt/2 power
a	3 minutes	a	45 seconds
b	6 minutes	b	3½ minutes
c	8-12 minutes	c	6-8 minutes
d	3 minutes	d	1½ minutes

	650 watt	
a	PL.7 for 1 minute	
b	PL.9 for 3½ minutes	
c	PL.7 for 7-10 minutes	
d	PL.8 for 2 minutes	

Curry

Cooking container: 2 pint casserole
Cooking time: 10 minutes
Number of servings: 4

1 can condensed lentil soup
1 peeled and sliced cooking apple
1 tablespoon (15 ml) coconut
¼ pint (150 ml) stock
curry powder or paste to taste
1 tablespoon (15 ml) raisins

Combine all ingredients and heat for [a] 6 minutes. Check seasoning. Heat for a further [b] 4 minutes, add cooked meat, vegetables or eggs and heat until warm. This curry sauce can be added to meat, vegetables or eggs.

	500 watt		650 watt/2 power
a	10 minutes	a	5 minutes
b	5 minutes	b	3 minutes

	650 watt	
a	PL.8 for 5½ minutes	
b	PL.8 for 3½ minutes	

Temp Probe: **a & b** H & H 80°C for 5 minutes

Ham Joint P.169

Honolulu Baked Beans

Cooking container: 2½ pint casserole
Cooking time: 10 minutes
Number of servings: 3-4

15¾ oz. (447 g) tin baked beans
12 oz. (340 g) luncheon meat (cubed)
small tin of pineapple chunks

Combine all ingredients, cover and heat until hot [a] 10 minutes. Stir before serving.

500 watt		650 watt/2 power	
a	12 minutes	a	8 minutes
650 watt			
a	PL.8 for 10 minutes		

Temp Probe: **a** H & H 85°C for 5 minutes

South of the Border

Cooking container: 3 pint dish
Cooking time: 29 minutes
Number of servings: 4

1 packet Spanish rice mix or savoury rice
14 oz. (397 g) can tomatoes
6 stuffed green olives, sliced
4 slices uncooked bacon
½ pint (300 ml) hot water

Cook bacon until crisp approximately [a] 5 minutes. Combine rice, water and tomatoes in a 3 pint dish. Cook loosely covered for [b] 24 minutes. Crumble the bacon and mix into the rice. Garnish with olives.

500 watt		650 watt/2 power	
a	5 minutes	a	4-5 minutes
b	25 minutes	b	22 minutes
650 watt			
a	PL.9 for 4-5 minutes		
b	PL.9 for 22 minutes		

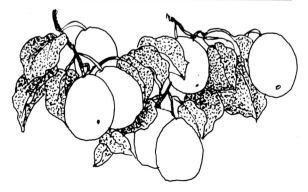

Chocolate Pear Upside Down Pudding

Cooking container: Soufflé dish
Cooking time: 7 minutes
Number of servings: 5-6

2 packets chocolate cake mix (use the small inexpensive size)
1 small can pear halves
3 tablespoons (45 ml) golden syrup

Mix the cake mixes as directed on the packet substituting water with the pear juice (add 2 tablespoons extra liquid). Grease a soufflé dish and place golden syrup in base of dish then pear halves, cover with cake mix. Cover with cling film, cook for [a] 7 minutes and leave to stand before turning out.

500 watt	650 watt/2 power	
Not suitable	a	6 minutes
650 watt		
a	PL.9 for 6 minutes	

Apple Flan

Cooking container: Serving dish
Cooking time: 4 minutes
Number of servings: 4

1 x 5" - 6" flan case, pre-cooked
2 tablespoons (30 ml) blackberry jam
stewed sweetened apples
good pinch cinnamon
chopped nuts

Place flan case into serving dish. Spread jam over base. Top with stewed apples — sprinkle with cinnamon and chopped nuts. Heat for [a] 4 minutes. Delicious hot with cream or custard.

500 watt		650 watt/2 power	
a	5 minutes	a	3 minutes
650 watt			
a	PL.8 for 3¾ minutes		

Cherry Cheese Pie

Cooking container: Flan dish
Cooking time: 3 minutes
Number of servings: 5

1 packet crushed pink wafer biscuits
2½ oz. (65 g) butter
6 oz. (175 g) curd cheese
1 egg
1½ oz. (35 g) caster sugar
½ teaspoon (2.5 ml) almond essence
1 can cherry pie filling

Melt butter in oven for [a] 1 minute. Mix with crushed wafer biscuits. Line base of flan dish with this. Soften cheese for [b] 2 minutes on defrost. Beat in sugar, egg and essence and spread mixture over the biscuit base. Cover with cherry pie filling.

	500 watt			650 watt/2 power
a	1½ minutes		a	30 seconds
b	3½ minutes on defrost		b	2 minutes on defrost
	650 watt			
	a	PL.7 for 1 minute		
	b	PL.3 for 2 minutes		

Quick Fruit Crumble

Cooking container: 8" shallow dish
Cooking time: 9 minutes
Number of servings: 4-5

1 x 14 oz. (397 g) can Blackberry & Apple pie filling
8 oz. (227 g) mix of crumble

Into an 8" round shallow dish empty fruit filling. Top with crumble. Cook in oven for [a] 9 minutes. For a golden topping place under grill or top with finely chopped or crushed nuts. Some bubbling of the fruit mixture through the crumble may occur.

	500 watt		650 watt/2 power
a	11 minutes	a	8 minutes
	650 watt		
	a	PL.9 for 8 minutes	

Mincemeat Flan

Cooking container: Flan dish
Cooking time: 6½ minutes
Number of servings: 5-6

2½ oz. (65 g) butter
1 packet lightly crushed Boudoir biscuits
5 heaped tablespoons (75 ml) mincemeat
2 tablespoons (30 ml) sweet white wine
pinch rosemary

Melt butter in the oven for [a] 1½ minutes then stir in crushed biscuits. Line base and sides of flan dish with this. Mix mincemeat with wine and rosemary and spread over biscuit base. Cook uncovered for [b] 5 minutes and serve with cream.

	500 watt			650 watt/2 power
a	2 minutes		a	1 minute
b	6 minutes		b	4½ minutes
	650 watt			
	a	PL.7 for 1½ minutes		
	b	PL.8 for 4¾ minutes		

Cherries & Pears in Wine Sauce

Cooking container: 2 pint bowl
Cooking time: 5 minutes
Number of servings: 4

15 oz. (425 g) can cherries
15 oz. (425 g) can pears
2 fl. oz. (50 ml) sweet white wine
2 tablespoons (30 ml) cornflour

Drain the juice from the fruit into a 2 pint bowl. Mix a little of this juice with the cornflour until smooth. Add the remaining juice and the wine. Heat for [a] 5 minutes, stir well twice during this cycle. Stir in the fruit and serve on its own or as a topping to ice cream.

	500 watt		650 watt/2 power
a	6½-7 minutes	a	4½ minutes
	650 watt		
	a	PL.9 for 4½ minutes	

Notes:

Recipes	Page No:	My Timing	Recipes	Page No:	My Timing

Meals for One

Meals for One

With a microwave oven in the kitchen, cooking for one is no longer the chore which leads many of us to eat snacks of dubious nutritional value or reach for the nearest biscuit. The time and effort needed to think up, prepare, cook, eat and wash up just for yourself often doesn't seem worthwhile. The microwave oven will cut down on all that and make meals enjoyable when cooking for one.

The recipes in this section are for one person but most of the meat, fish and vegetable recipes in other sections can be cut down and timed using these as a guideline.

Microwave method to preparing a meal for one

1 Cook potatoes first.
2 Cook meat or fish.
3 Reheat vegetables if required before serving.

Browning Dish Breakfast

Cooking container: Browning dish
Cooking time: 2 minutes
Number of servings: 1

2 rashers of bacon
1 egg

Heat browning dish for [a] 4 minutes, place the bacon onto it and cook for [b] 1 minute. Turn bacon over and break egg into the centre of the dish. Cover with lid and cook for a further [c] minute.

	500 watt		650 watt/2 power
a	4 minutes	a	4 minutes
b	1 minute	b	1 minute
c	1 minute	c	30 seconds

	650 watt
a	PL.8 for 4 minutes
b	PL.8 for 1 minute
c	PL.8 for 1 minute

Browning Dish Breakfast

174

Gammon Steak Special

Cooking container: Serving dish
Cooking time: 7 minutes
Number of servings: 1

12 oz. (350 g) thick gammon steak
1 tablespoon (15 ml) marmalade
1 teaspoon (5 g) lemon juice

Cut gammon steak in half lengthways and snip edges.
Place on dish and cook for [a] 3 minutes. Drain off juice,
cover with one heaped tablespoon marmalade mixed
with a little lemon juice and cook for [b] 4-6 minutes.
Allow to stand for 2 minutes before serving.

500 watt		650 watt/2 power	
a	3 minutes	a	1½ minutes
b	4-6 minutes	b	2-4 minutes
650 watt			
a	PL.9 for 1½ minutes		
b	PL.9 for 2-4 minutes		

Hamburger Special

Cooking container: Serving dish
Cooking time: 2 minutes
Number of servings: 1

1 x 4 oz. (100 g) hamburger (if frozen, defrost)
2 teaspoons (10 ml) chutney
good pinch of mustard
good pinch of brown sugar

Mix the chutney, mustard and brown sugar together and
spread over the hamburger. Cook for [a] 1½-2 minutes.
Serve with a salad and hot bread roll.

500 watt		650 watt/2 power	
a	2½-3 minutes	a	1-1½ minutes
650 watt			
a	PL.9 for 1-1½ minutes		

Chicken Kiev

Cooking container: Serving plate
Cooking time: 5 minutes
Number of servings: 1

10 oz. (275 g) chicken breast, boned and flattened
1 oz. (25 g) butter mixed with parsley or garlic
1 small bread roll — made into breadcrumbs
1 beaten egg
chicken seasoning

Form the butter into an oblong and lay on chicken
breast, fold around and secure with wooden cocktail
sticks. Dip chicken into beaten egg. Roll in breadcrumbs
mixed with chicken seasoning. Set in fridge for 1 hour.
Dip in egg and roll again in breadcrumbs. Place on
serving plate and cook for [a] 2 minutes. Turn and cook
for a further [b] 3-4 minutes. Rest for 2 minutes before
eating.

500 watt		650 watt/2 power	
a	2 minutes	a	1½ minutes
b	3 minutes	b	2½-3 minutes
650 watt			
a	PL.7 for 2 minutes		
b	PL.7 for 3-4 minutes		

Quickie Casserole

Cooking container: 1 pint casserole
Cooking time: 7 minutes
Number of servings: 1

4 Frankfurters cut into chunks
4 oz. (100 g) baked beans
good pinch mustard
1 teaspoon (5 ml) Worcestershire sauce

Combine all ingredients into a 1 pint casserole dish. Heat
for [a] 3 minutes. Stir and heat for a further [b] 4
minutes.

500 watt		650 watt/2 power	
a	5 minutes	a	2½ minutes
b	5 minutes	b	2 minutes
650 watt			
a	PL.8 for 3 minutes		
b	PL.8 for 2 minutes		

Temp Probe: **a** 60°C, PL.8, stir
b 85°C, PL.8

Haddock with Prawns

Cooking container: Serving plate
Cooking time: 2 minutes
Number of servings: 1

4 oz. (100 g) haddock
butter
salt and pepper
2 oz. (50 g) prawns

Place the haddock on serving plate, dot with butter, season lightly, cover and cook for [a] 1 minute. Add the prawns, cover and heat for [b] 30 seconds.

	500 watt		650 watt/2 power	
a	1½ minutes	a	45 seconds
b	1 minute	b	45 seconds
	650 watt			
	a	PL.9 for 45 secs 1-minute		
	b	PL.9 for 45 seconds		

Baked Apple with Mincemeat

See colour plate page 177

Cooking container: Sweet bowl
Cooking time: 2 minutes
Number of servings: 1

5 oz. (125 g) cooking apple, cored
mincemeat

Fill the apple with mincemeat, place in the sweet bowl and cook for [a] 2 minutes. Stand before serving.

	500 watt		650 watt/2 power
a	3 minutes	a	1½-2 minutes
	650 watt		
	a	PL.9 for 1½ minutes	

Liver with Bacon & Onions

Cooking container: Browning dish
Cooking time: 5½-6 minutes
Number of servings: 1

6 oz. (175 g) calves liver
2 rashers bacon, chopped
½ small onion, chopped
salt and pepper

Heat browning dish for [a] 5 minutes. Add bacon and onion and cook for [b] 1½ minutes. Add liver, season lightly and cook for [c] 2 minutes. Turn over and cook for a further [d] 2 minutes. Serve with jacket potato.

	500 watt		650 watt/2 power
a	6 minutes	a	4 minutes
b	1½ minutes	b	1 minute
c	2 minutes	c	1 minute
d	2-3 minutes	d	1½-2 minutes
	650 watt		
	a	PL.8 for 5 minutes	
	b	PL.8 for 1 minute	
	c	PL.8 for 1½ minutes	
	d	PL.8 for 2-3 minutes	

Liver with Bacon & Onions

Lemony Chicken

Cooking container: Greaseproof paper
Cooking time: 8 minutes
Number of servings: 1

1 x 8 oz. (225 g) chicken portion
chicken seasoning
2 teaspoons (10 ml) honey
2 teaspoons (10 ml) lemon juice
butter

Rub the chicken portion with butter. Place on a large sheet of greaseproof paper, sprinkle with chicken seasoning and pour honey and lemon over chicken. Wrap in paper and cook on defrost for [a] 3 minutes. Turn over and cook for a further [b] 5 minutes on defrost power. Stand covered for 2 minutes before serving.

	500 watt		650 watt/2 power
a	4 minutes on defrost	a	3 minutes on defrost
b	6 minutes on defrost	b	5 minutes on defrost
	650 watt		
	a	PL.4 for 3 minutes	
	b	PL.4 for 5 minutes	

Corn-on-the-Cob

Cooking container: Greaseproof paper
Cooking time: 5 minutes
Number of servings: 1

Frozen corn on the cob
butter
salt and pepper

Place the cob on greaseproof paper, dot with butter and sprinkle with salt and pepper. Wrap in paper and cook for [a] 5 minutes.

	500 watt		650 watt/2 power
a	6 minutes	a	4½ minutes
	650 watt		
	a	PL.9 for 4½ minutes	

Pork Chop with Apple

Cooking container: Browning dish
Cooking time: 8½ minutes
Number of servings: 1

6 oz. (175 g) pork chop
4 oz. (100 g) eating apple, cored and sliced

Heat browning dish for [a] 5 minutes. Season chop and press onto dish with sliced apples. Cook for [b] 2 minutes. Turn and cook for a further [c] 1½ minutes. Apples can be lightly buttered before cooking if desired.

	500 watt		650 watt/2 power
a	6 minutes	a	5 minutes
b	2 minutes	b	1½ minutes
c	2 minutes	c	1 minute
	650 watt		
	a	PL.8 for 5 minutes	
	b	PL.8 for 2 minutes	
	c	PL.8 for 1½ minutes	

Corn-on-the-Cob

178

Dieting

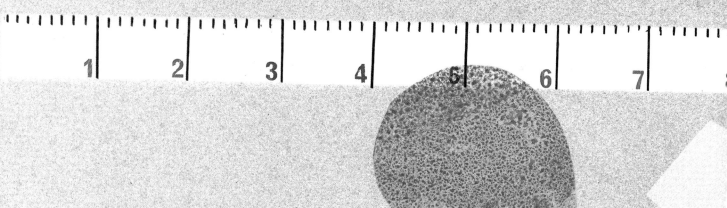

Dieting

Calorie Count

Trying to lose weight is no easy matter. Watching the family tuck into meat pies and cakes makes it almost impossible to eat salads and not leave the table feeling hungry, particularly on cold days. To prepare special slimming meals for one can present problems but with the help of the microwave oven you will find it is no effort at all. Your microwave oven will help you prepare slimmers food quickly and economically. Remember too, that more essential nutrients are left in the food.

The recipes have not been written as part of a rigid diet plan — they are just to give you an idea of the simplicity of doing calorie counted recipes with the microwave oven.

Where bread or toast is mentioned the calorie count is for one slice of wholemeal bread weighing approximately 1 oz. Where buttered toast is mentioned, then ½ oz. low calorie spread has been used and counted in the total calorie count.

Porridge

Cooking container: Cereal bowl
Cooking time: 5 minutes
Number of servings: 1

1 oz. (25 g) porridge
7 fl. oz. (240 ml) water
pinch salt

Combine all ingredients in bowl and cook for [a] 4-5 minutes in the microwave oven. Stir twice during cooking cycle.

Calorie count: 115

	500 watt		650 watt/2 power
a	5-6 minutes	a	3-4 minutes
650 watt			
a	PL.7 for 4-5 minutes		

Scrambled Eggs

Cooking container: 1 pint pyrex jug
Cooking time: 2 minutes
Number of servings: 1

2 eggs size 2
seasoning
1 tablespoon (15 ml) water
½ oz (15 g) low calorie spread

Combine all ingredients in pyrex jug. Cook to required thickness approximately [a] 1-2 minutes and stir before serving.

Calorie count: 240

	500 watt		650 watt/2 power
a	1-2 minutes	a	1-2 minutes
650 watt			
a	PL.9 for 1-2 minutes		

Poached egg

Cooking container: small dish
Cooking time: 45 seconds
Number of servings: 1

1 egg size 2
2 tablespoons (30 ml) cold water
slice buttered toast

Put cold water in small dish. Break in the egg, prick with a skewer and cook for [a] 45 seconds. Stand to finish cooking. Serve on toast.

Calorie count: 215

	500 watt		650 watt/2 power
a	45 secs – 1 min	a	45 seconds
650 watt			
a	PL.5 for 1½ minutes		

Tomato Soup

Cooking container: 4 pint casserole
Cooking time: 18 minutes
Number of servings: 3-4

1 stick celery, finely chopped
12 fl. oz. (350 ml) tomato juice
1 sachet bouquet garni
½ pint water (275 ml)
1 chicken stock cube
seasoning to taste

Cook celery for [a] 2 minutes and add all other ingredients. Cook uncovered for [b] 16 minutes. Remove bouquet garni and serve.

Calorie count: 124

	500 watt		650 watt/2 power
a	3 minutes	a	1½ minutes
b	20 minutes	b	15 minutes
650 watt			
a	PL.7 for 2 minutes		
b	PL.7 for 16 minutes		

Cauliflower soup

Cooking container: 2½ pint casserole
Cooking time: 17 minutes
Number of servings: 3-4

12 oz (350 g) cauliflower
¾ pint (425 ml) hot water
1 chicken stock cube
1 bay leaf
1 teaspoon minced onion
seasoning to taste

Combine all ingredients and cook covered for [a] 17 minutes. Remove bay leaf, puree and heat before serving.

Calorie count: 76

	500 watt		650 watt/2 power
a	20 minutes	a	15 minutes
650 watt			
a	PL.9 for 15 minutes		

Prawn & Cucumber

See colour plate page 183
Cooking container: 1 pint casserole
Cooking time: 6 minutes
Number of servings: 1

4 oz. (100 g) frozen prawns
½ chicken stock cube
¼ pint (150 ml) water
salt
4 oz. (100 g) cubed cucumber
2 oz (50 g) sliced mushrooms
1 slice wholemeal toast
½ oz. (15 g) low calorie spread

Cook cucumber and mushrooms, chicken stock and salt in the water in a covered container for [a] 3 minutes. Add prawns and cook for a further [b] 3 minutes. Drain and serve on hot toast.

Calorie count: 238

	500 watt		650 watt/2 power
a	4½ minutes	a	2½ minutes
b	4 minutes	b	2 minutes
650 watt			
a	PL.9 for 2½ minutes		
b	PL.8 for 3 minutes		

Cheese on Toast

Cooking container: Plate
Cooking time: 1 minute
Number of servings: 1

2 oz. (50 g) cheese, grated
1 slice buttered toast

Grate the cheese onto toast. Place on absorbent paper on plate and heat for [a] 1½ minutes. Serve.

Calorie count: 345

500 watt		650 watt/2 power	
a	1¾ minutes	a	1 minute
650 watt			
a	PL.7 for 1½ minutes		

Sardines on Toast

Cooking container: Plate
Cooking time: 45 seconds
Number of servings: 1

1 can sardines
1 slice toast (buttered with low calorie spread)

Drain oil from sardines and heat 2 oz. on toast placed on absorbent paper on a plate for [a] 45 seconds.

Calorie count: 235

500 watt		650 watt/2 power	
a	1 minutes	a	30 seconds
650 watt			
a	PL.7 for 45 seconds		

Stuffed Tomatoes

See colour plate page 183

Cooking container: Serving plate
Cooking time: 3 minutes
Number of servings: 1

3 oz. (75 g) drained tuna fish
2 large tomatoes
1 pinch salt, parsley, celery salt and minced onion
1 teaspoon (5 ml) Worcestershire Sauce

Slice top off tomatoes, scoop out centre and mix with all other ingredients. Fill tomatoes and heat for [a] 3 minutes.

Calorie count: 253

500 watt		650 watt/2 power	
a	4½ minutes	a	2½ minutes
650 watt			
a	PL.8 for 3 minutes		

Stuffed Tomatoes

Plaice with prawns

Cooking container: Serving dish
Cooking time: 4 minutes
Number of servings: 1

5 oz. (150 g) plaice
2 oz. (50 g) frozen prawns
salt to taste
lemon juice

Season the plaice with salt and lemon juice. Roll up with frozen prawns inside and cook covered on serving dish for [a] 4 minutes. Sprinkle with parsley before serving.

Calorie count: 172

500 watt		650 watt/2 power	
a	5 minutes	a	3½ minutes
650 watt			
	a	PL.9 for 3½ minutes	

Lamb Fillet

Cooking container: Browning dish
Cooking time: 4 minutes
Number of servings: 1

5 oz. (150 g) lamb fillet
¼ oz. (7 g) low calorie spread
seasoning

Smear lamb lightly with low calorie spread, season and cook on preheated browning dish for [a] 3-4 minutes.

Calorie count: 354

500 watt		650 watt/2 power	
a	4-5 minutes	a	3-4 minutes
650 watt			
	a	PL.8 for 3-4 minutes	

Oriental Sole

Cooking container: Serving dish
Cooking time: 3 minutes
Number of servings: 1

8 oz. (225 g) sole (weight including bone)
1 teaspoon (5 ml) soy sauce
1 teaspoon (5 ml) lemon juice
1 teaspoon (5 ml) tomato juice
1 pinch ground ginger
salt to taste

Place sole on serving dish. Combine all other ingredients and pour over fish. Cover and cook for [a] 3-3½ minutes.

Calorie count: 160

500 watt		650 watt/2 power	
a	3½-4½ minutes	a	2½-3 minutes
650 watt			
	a	PL. 9 for 2½-3 minutes	

Chicken

Cooking container: Browning dish
Cooking time: 4 minutes
Number of servings: 1

7 oz. (200 g) chicken portion
¼ oz. (7 g) low calorie spread
seasoning of your choice

Heat browning dish for [a] 5 minutes. Spread chicken with the low calorie spread and season. Cook for [b] approximately 4 minutes, turning as required.

Calorie count: 300

500 watt		650 watt/2 power	
a	6 minutes	a	5 minutes
b	6 minutes	b	4 minutes
650 watt			
	a	PL.8 for 6 minutes	
	b	PL.8 for 4 minutes	

Savoury Cod

See colour plate page 183
Cooking container: Serving dish
Cooking time: 3 minutes
Number of servings: 1

7 oz. (200 g) cod fillet
1 good pinch mustard powder
salt and pepper
1 pinch tarragon
1 teaspoon (5 ml) lemon juice
1 teaspoon (5 ml) water
paprika to taste

Lay fish on serving dish. Combine all other ingredients and spread over fish. Cook covered for [a] 2½-3 minutes.

Calorie count: 161

500 watt		650 watt/2 power	
a	3½-4½ minutes	a	2½ minutes
650 watt			
	a	PL.9 for 2½ minutes	

Steak

Cooking container: Browning dish
Cooking time: 1½ minutes
Number of servings: 1

7 oz. (200 g) steak
seasoned salt
¼ oz. (7 g) low calorie spread
pepper to taste

Heat browning dish for [a] 6 minutes. Smear steak with the low calorie spread and sprinkle with seasoning. Press onto the browning dish and cook for [b] 1½ minutes. Turn meat over and cook as required.

Calorie count: 430

500 watt		650 watt/2 power	
a	7 minutes	a	6 minutes
b	2 minutes	b	1 minute
650 watt			
	a	PL.8 for 6 minutes	
	b	PL.8 for 1½ minutes	

Sweet & Sour Pork

See colour plate page 183
Cooking container: Browning dish
Cooking time: 4½ minutes
Number of servings: 1

6 oz. (175 g) pork fillet
2 teaspoons (10 ml) low calorie orange squash
2 teaspoon (10 ml) soy sauce
1 tablespoon (15 ml) tomato juice
1 pinch artificial sweetener

Heat browning dish for [a] 4½ minutes. Press on meat and cook for [b] 1 minute. Turn meat over and cook for a further minute. Combine all other ingredients, pour over meat and cook for [c] 2½ minutes.

Calorie count: 380

500 watt		650 watt/2 power	
a	5 minutes	a	4 minutes
b	1½ minutes	b	45 seconds
c	3 minutes	c	2 minutes
650 watt			
	a	PL.9 for 4 minutes	
	b	PL.8 for 1 minute	
	c	PL.8 for 2½ minutes	

Herb Liver Special

Cooking container: Browning skillet
Cooking time: 13½ minutes
Number of servings: 1

6 oz. (175 g) liver
1 sliced tomato
¼ finely sliced green pepper
1 pinch rosemary
salt and pepper
3 tablespoons (75 ml) tomato juice
1 pinch parsley
1 pinch minced onion
low calorie margarine

Heat browning dish for [a] 5 minutes. Smear liver with margarine and press onto dish. Cook for [b] 1½ minutes. Turn liver onto other side, add all other ingredients, cover with lid and cook for [c] 12 minutes on defrost power.

Calorie count: 320

	500 watt		650 watt/2 power
a	6 minutes	a	5 minutes
b	2 minutes	b	1 minute
c	10 minutes full power	c	10-12 mintues on defrost
650 watt			
a	PL.8 for 5 minutes		
b	PL.8 for 1½ minutes		
c	PL.4 for 12 minutes		

Baked Apple with Rum

Cooking container: Sweet bowl
Cooking time: 3 minutes
Number of servings: 1

1 cored apple (5 oz.) (150 g)
1 tablespoon (15 ml) water mixed with artificial sweetener
rum essence to taste

Pour liquid over apple and cook for [a] 3 minutes. Leave to stand for 3 minutes before serving. (Note: Cooking time will vary depending on type of apple).

Calorie count: 45

	500 watt		650 watt/2 power
a	4 minutes	a	2½ minutes
650 watt			
a	PL.7 for 3 minutes		

Banana Favourite

Cooking container: Sweet bowl
Cooking time: 1 minute
Number of servings: 1

1 sliced banana
2 tablespoons (30 ml) low calorie orange squash
pinch cinnamon

Place all ingredients into a sweet bowl, cover and heat for [a] 1 minute.

Calorie count: 88

	500 watt		650 watt/2 power
a	1½ minutes	a	45 seconds
650 watt			
a	PL.7 for 1 minute		

Grape Jelly

Cooking container: 1 pint dish
Cooking time: 1½ minutes
Number of servings: 2

1 can one-calorie lemon and lime drink
1 packet gelatine
5 oz. (150 g) grapes

Heat gelatine with 6 tablespoons of the lemon and lime drink for [a] 1-1½ minutes or until the gelatine has dissolved. Stir well. Add the remaining liquid and grapes. Leave to set.

Calorie count: 125

	500 watt		650 watt/2 power
a	1½-2½ minutes	a	1 minute approx.
650 watt			
a	PL.7 for 1-1½ minutes		

Gingered Pear

Cooking container: Cereal bowl
Cooking time: 1 minute
Number of servings: 1

1 pear, halved and peeled
5 fl. oz. (150 ml) slimline ginger ale
artificial sweetener to taste

Place all ingredients into a cereal bowl and cook for [a]
1½ minutes.

Calorie count: 40

500 watt		650 watt/2 power	
a	2 minutes	a	1 minute
650 watt			
	a	PL.9 for 1 minute	

Cranberry Special

Cooking container: Cereal bowl
Cooking time: 3 minutes
Number of servings: 1

4 oz. (100 g) cranberries
3 fl. oz. (90 ml) low calorie orange squash
artificial sweetener to taste

Mix all ingredients in cereal bowl and cook for [a] 3
minutes. Stir and serve.

Calorie count: 12

500 watt		650 watt/2 power	
a	4 minutes	a	2½ minutes
650 watt			
	a	PL.9 for 2½ minutes	

Notes:

Recipes	Page No:	My Timing

Recipes	Page No:	My Timing

Index